Criminal Justice (Scotland) Act 2(

2003 asp 7

ISBN 0 10 590049 4

CORRECTION

Page 74 –

Section **76** (4)(c)

Amend reference to new subsection "(5)" to read new subsection "(8)"

September 2003

PRINTED IN THE UNITED KINGDOM BY THE STATIONERY OFFICE LIMITED
under the authority and superintendence of Carol Tullo, the Queen's Printer for Scotland

Criminal Justice (Scotland) Act 2003
2003 asp 7

CONTENTS

Section

PART 3

SEXUAL OFFENCES ETC.

PART 4

PRISONERS ETC.

Custody and temporary detention

Consecutive sentences

Release of prisoners

Special provision as regards certain life prisoners

Monitoring on release

Parole Board to have regard to risk management plans

PART 5

DRUGS COURTS

PART 6

NON-CUSTODIAL PUNISHMENTS

PART 7

CHILDREN

PART 8

EVIDENTIAL, JURISDICTIONAL AND PROCEDURAL MATTERS

Evidential matters

Jurisdictional matters

Procedural matters

PART 9

BRIBERY AND CORRUPTION

Criminal Justice (Scotland) Act 2003
2003 asp 7

The Bill for this Act of the Scottish Parliament was passed by the Parliament on 20th February 2003 and received Royal Assent on 26th March 2003

An Act of the Scottish Parliament to make provision in relation to criminal justice, criminal procedure and evidence in criminal proceedings; to make provision as to the arrest, sentencing, custody and release of offenders and the obtaining of reports in relation to offenders; to make provision for the provision of assistance by local authorities to persons who are arrested and are in police custody or who are subject to a deferred sentence and for the making of grants to local authorities exercising jointly certain functions in relation to offenders and other persons; to make provision for the protection of the public at large from persons with a propensity to commit certain offences and for the establishment of the Risk Management Authority; to make provision for the granting of certain rights to the victims of crime; to make provision as to the jurisdiction of courts and the designation of certain courts as drugs courts; to make provision in relation to the physical punishment of children; to create offences in connection with traffic in prostitution or for purposes connected with pornography; to make provision as to the criminal law as it relates to bribery and the acceptance of bribes; to make provision in relation to criminal legal assistance; to require the aggravation of an offence by religious prejudice to be taken into account in sentencing; to make provision as respects police ranks and the powers and duties of certain civilians employed by police authorities; to make provision for the disqualification of convicted persons from jury service in both criminal and civil proceedings and for the separation of juries after retiral; to make provision for the use of live television links between prisons and courts; to make provision in relation to warrants to search; to amend Part V of the Police Act 1997 in its application to Scotland; to make provision in relation to the prohibition of certain matters in respect of cases referred to the Principal Reporter; to amend the law relating to penalties for wildlife offences; and for connected purposes.

PART 1

PROTECTION OF THE PUBLIC AT LARGE

Risk assessment and order for lifelong restriction

1   Risk assessment and order for lifelong restriction

(1)   In Part XI of the 1995 Act (sentencing), after section 210AA (which is inserted into that Act by section 20 of this Act) there is inserted—

"Risk assessment

210B   Risk assessment order

(1)   This subsection applies where it falls to the High Court to impose sentence on a person convicted of an offence other than murder and that offence—

(a)   is (any or all)—

(i)   a sexual offence (as defined in section 210A(10) of this Act);

(ii)   a violent offence (as so defined);

(iii)   an offence which endangers life; or

(b)   is an offence the nature of which, or circumstances of the commission of which, are such that it appears to the court that the person has a propensity to commit any such offence as is mentioned in sub-paragraphs (i) to (iii) of paragraph (a) above.

(2)   Where subsection (1) above applies, the court, at its own instance or (provided that the prosecutor has given the person notice of his intention in that regard) on the motion of the prosecutor, if it considers that the risk criteria may be met, shall make an order under this subsection (a "risk assessment order") unless—

(a)   the court makes an interim hospital order by virtue of section 210D(1) of this Act in respect of the person; or

(b)   the person is subject to an order for lifelong restriction previously imposed.

(3)   A risk assessment order is an order—

(a)   for the convicted person to be taken to a place specified in the order, so that there may be prepared there—

(i)   by a person accredited for the purposes of this section by the Risk Management Authority; and

(ii)   in such manner as may be so accredited,

a risk assessment report (that is to say, a report as to what risk his being at liberty presents to the safety of the public at large); and

(b)   providing for him to be remanded in custody there for so long as is necessary for those purposes and thereafter there or elsewhere until such diet as is fixed for sentence.

(4)   On making a risk assessment order, the court shall adjourn the case for a period not exceeding ninety days.

(5)   The court may on one occasion, on cause shown, extend the period mentioned in subsection (4) above by not more than ninety days; and it may exceptionally, where by reason of circumstances outwith the control of the person to whom it falls to prepare the risk assessment report (the "assessor"), or as the case may be of any person instructed under section 210C(5) of this Act to prepare such a report, the report in question has not been completed, grant such further extension as appears to it to be appropriate.

(6)   There shall be no appeal against a risk assessment order or against any refusal to make such an order.

210C   Risk assessment report

(1)   The assessor may, in preparing the risk assessment report, take into account not only any previous conviction of the convicted person but also any allegation that the person has engaged in criminal behaviour (whether or not that behaviour resulted in prosecution and acquittal).

(2)   Where the assessor, in preparing the risk assessment report, takes into account any allegation that the person has engaged in criminal behaviour, the report is to—

   (a)   list each such allegation;

   (b)   set out any additional evidence which supports the allegation; and

   (c)   explain the extent to which the allegation and evidence has influenced the opinion included in the report under subsection (3) below.

(3)   The assessor shall include in the risk assessment report his opinion as to whether the risk mentioned in section 210B(3)(a) of this Act is, having regard to such standards and guidelines as are issued by the Risk Management Authority in that regard, high, medium or low.

(4)   The assessor shall submit the risk assessment report to the High Court by sending it, together with such documents as are available to the assessor and are referred to in the report, to the Principal Clerk of Justiciary, who shall then send a copy of the report and of those documents to the prosecutor and to the convicted person.

(5)   The convicted person may, during the period of his detention at the place specified in the risk assessment order, himself instruct the preparation (by a person other than the assessor) of a risk assessment report; and if such a report is so prepared then the person who prepares it shall submit it to the court by sending it, together with such documents as are available to him (after any requirement under subsection (4) above is met) and are referred to in the report, to the Principal Clerk of Justiciary, who shall then send a copy of it and of those documents to the prosecutor.

(6)   When the court receives the risk assessment report submitted by the assessor a diet shall be fixed for the convicted person to be brought before it for sentence.

(7)   If, within such period after receiving a copy of that report as may be prescribed by Act of Adjournal, the convicted person intimates, in such form, or as nearly as may be in such form, as may be so prescribed—

   (a)   that he objects to the content or findings of that report; and

   (b)   what the grounds of his objection are,

   the prosecutor and he shall be entitled to produce and examine witnesses with regard to—

   (i)   that content or those findings; and

   (ii)   the content or findings of any risk assessment report instructed by the person and duly submitted under subsection (5) above.

210D   Interim hospital order and assessment of risk

(1)   Where subsection (1) of section 210B of this Act applies, the High Court, if—

(a) it may make an interim hospital order in respect of the person under section 53 of this Act; and

(b) it considers that the risk criteria may be met,

shall make such an order unless the person is subject to an order for lifelong restriction previously imposed.

(2) Where an interim hospital order is made by virtue of subsection (1) above, a report as to the risk the convicted person's being at liberty presents to the safety of the public at large shall be prepared by a person accredited for the purposes of this section by the Risk Management Authority and in such manner as may be so accredited.

(3) Section 210C(1) to (4) and (7) (except paragraph (ii)) of this Act shall apply in respect of any such report as it does in respect of a risk assessment report.

210E   The risk criteria

For the purposes of sections 195(1), 210B(2), 210D(1) and 210F(1) and (3) of this Act, the risk criteria are that the nature of, or the circumstances of the commission of, the offence of which the convicted person has been found guilty either in themselves or as part of a pattern of behaviour are such as to demonstrate that there is a likelihood that he, if at liberty, will seriously endanger the lives, or physical or psychological well-being, of members of the public at large.

Order for lifelong restriction etc.

210F   Order for lifelong restriction

(1) The High Court, at its own instance or on the motion of the prosecutor, if it is satisfied, having regard to—

(a) a risk assessment report submitted under section 210C(4) or (5) of this Act;

(b) any report submitted by virtue of section 210D of this Act;

(c) any evidence given under section 210C(7) of this Act; and

(d) any other information before it,

that, on a balance of probabilities, the risk criteria are met, shall make an order for lifelong restriction in respect of the convicted person.

(2) An order for lifelong restriction constitutes a sentence of imprisonment, or as the case may be detention, for an indeterminate period.

(3) The prosecutor may, on the grounds that on a balance of probabilities the risk criteria are met, appeal against any refusal of the court to make an order for lifelong restriction.

210G   Disposal of case where certain orders not made

(1) Where, in respect of a convicted person—

(a) a risk assessment order is not made under section 210B(2) of this Act, or (as the case may be) an interim hospital order is not made by virtue of section 210D(1) of this Act, because the court does not consider that the risk criteria may be met; or

(b) the court considers that the risk criteria may be met but a risk assessment order, or (as the case may be) an interim hospital order, is not so made because the person is subject to an order for lifelong restriction previously imposed,

the court shall dispose of the case as it considers appropriate.

(2) Where, in respect of a convicted person, an order for lifelong restriction is not made under section 210F of this Act because the court is not satisfied (in accordance with subsection (1) of that section) that the risk criteria are met, the court, in disposing of the case, shall not impose on the person a sentence of imprisonment for life, detention for life or detention without limit of time.

Report of judge

210H Report of judge

(1) This subsection applies where a person falls to be sentenced—

(a) in the High Court for an offence (other than murder) mentioned in section 210B(1) of this Act; or

(b) in the sheriff court for such an offence prosecuted on indictment.

(2) Where subsection (1) above applies, the court shall, as soon as reasonably practicable, prepare a report in writing, in such form as may be prescribed by Act of Adjournal—

(a) as to the circumstances of the case; and

(b) containing such other information as it considers appropriate,

but no such report shall be prepared if a report is required to be prepared under section 21(4) of the Criminal Justice (Scotland) Act 2003 (asp 7).".

(2) Schedule 1, which contains amendments consequential upon the provisions of subsection (1), has effect.

Disposal in case of insanity

2 Disposal of case where accused found to be insane

In section 57 (disposal of case where accused found to be insane) of the 1995 Act—

(a) in subsection (2) after paragraph (b) there is inserted—

"(bb) make an interim hospital order;"; and

(b) for subsection (3) there is substituted—

"(3) Where the court is satisfied, having regard to a report submitted in respect of the person following an interim hospital order, that, on a balance of probabilities, the risk his being at liberty presents to the safety of the public at large is high, it shall make orders under both paragraphs (a) and (b) of subsection (2) above in respect of that person.".

The Risk Management Authority

3   The Risk Management Authority

(1)   There is established an authority (to be known as the "Risk Management Authority") whose functions under this Act and any other enactment are to be exercised for the purpose of ensuring the effective assessment and minimisation of risk.

(2)   For the purposes of subsection (1) and sections 4 to 6, "risk" means, as regards—

(a)   a person convicted of an offence; or

(b)   a person who is subject to a disposal under section 57 (disposal of case where accused found to be insane) of the 1995 Act,

the risk the person's being at liberty presents to the safety of the public at large.

(3)   Schedule 2 has effect with respect to the Authority.

4   Policy and research

In, or as the case may be in relation to, the assessment and minimisation of risk—

(a)   the Risk Management Authority is to—

(i)   compile and keep under review information about the provision of services in Scotland;

(ii)   compile and keep under review research and development;

(iii) promote effective practice; and

(iv)   give such advice and make such recommendations to the Scottish Ministers as it considers appropriate; and

(b)   the Authority may—

(i)   carry out, commission or co-ordinate research and publish the results of such research; and

(ii)   undertake pilot schemes for the purposes of developing and improving methods.

5   Guidelines and standards

(1)   The Risk Management Authority is to—

(a)   prepare and issue guidelines as to the assessment and minimisation of risk; and

(b)   set and publish standards according to which measures taken in respect of the assessment and minimisation of risk are to be judged.

(2)   Any person having functions in relation to the assessment and minimisation of risk is to have regard to such guidelines and standards in the exercise of those functions.

6   Risk management plans

(1)   A plan (a "risk management plan") must be prepared in respect of—

(a)   any offender who is subject to an order for lifelong restriction made under section 210F (order for lifelong restriction) of the 1995 Act; and

(b)   any offender falling within such other category as may be prescribed.

(2) Before making an order by virtue of subsection (1)(b), the Scottish Ministers are to consult—

   (a) the Risk Management Authority; and

   (b) such other persons as they consider appropriate.

(3) The risk management plan must—

   (a) set out an assessment of risk;

   (b) set out the measures to be taken for the minimisation of risk, and how such measures are to be co-ordinated; and

   (c) be in such form as is specified under subsection (5).

(4) The risk management plan may provide for any person who may reasonably be expected to assist in the minimisation of risk to have functions in relation to the implementation of the plan.

(5) The Risk Management Authority is to specify and publish the form of risk management plans.

(6) The Risk Management Authority may issue guidance (either generally or in a particular case) as to the preparation, implementation or review of any risk management plan.

7 Preparation of risk management plans

(1) Where the offender is serving a sentence—

   (a) of imprisonment in a prison;

   (b) of detention in a young offenders institution; or

   (c) by virtue of section 208 (detention of children convicted on indictment) of the 1995 Act, of detention in some other place,

the risk management plan is to be prepared by the Scottish Ministers.

(2) Where the offender is detained (or liable to be detained) in a hospital by virtue of—

   (a) a hospital order under section 58 (order for hospital admission or guardianship) of the 1995 Act;

   (b) a hospital direction under section 59A (hospital directions) of the 1995 Act;

   (c) an application for admission under Part V (admission to hospital etc.) of the Mental Health (Scotland) Act 1984 (c.36) ("the 1984 Act"); or

   (d) a transfer direction under section 71 (removal to hospital of prisoners) of the 1984 Act,

the risk management plan is to be prepared by the managers of the hospital in which the offender is detained (or liable to be detained).

(3) Where the risk management plan does not require to be prepared by the Scottish Ministers or the managers of a hospital under subsections (1) and (2), the plan is to be prepared by the local authority in whose area the offender resides.

(4) In this section, the expressions "managers of a hospital" and "hospital" are to be construed in accordance with section 125 (interpretation) of the 1984 Act.

(5) Whoever is required by virtue of this section to prepare the risk management plan is referred to in sections 8 and 9 as the "lead authority".

8   Preparation of risk management plans: further provision

(1)   Preparation of the risk management plan is to be completed no later than 9 months after the offender is sentenced or detained (or becomes liable to be detained) in hospital; but if there is an appeal under subsection (7), it may be completed within such longer period as the Risk Management Authority may reasonably require.

(2)   In preparing the risk management plan, the lead authority is to consult—

        (a)   any person on whom, by virtue of section 6(4), the lead authority is considering conferring functions; and

        (b)   such other persons as it considers appropriate.

(3)   Any person so consulted is to provide such assistance to the lead authority as it may reasonably require for the purposes of preparing the plan.

(4)   The lead authority is to submit the risk management plan to the Risk Management Authority and the Risk Management Authority is to—

        (a)   approve it; or

        (b)   where it considers that a plan does not comply with section 6(3) or that the lead authority has, in preparing the plan, disregarded any guideline or standard under section 5 or any guidance under section 6(6), reject it.

(5)   Where any plan is rejected, the lead authority is to prepare a revised plan and submit it to the Risk Management Authority by such time as the Authority may reasonably require.

(6)   Where the Risk Management Authority—

        (a)   rejects a revised plan; and

        (b)   considers that, unless it exercises its power under this subsection to give directions, subsection (1) would not be complied with,

    the Authority may give directions to the lead authority and any other person having functions under the plan as to the preparation of a revised plan; and the lead authority and such other person must, subject to subsection (7), comply with any such direction.

(7)   The lead authority or any other person to whom any direction is given under subsection (6) may appeal to the sheriff against the direction on the grounds that it is unreasonable.

9   Implementation and review of risk management plans

(1)   The lead authority and any other person having functions under the risk management plan are to implement the plan in accordance with their respective functions.

(2)   Where the Risk Management Authority considers that the lead authority or any such other person is failing, without reasonable excuse, to implement the plan in accordance with those functions, the Authority may give directions to the lead authority or, as the case may be, the person as to the implementation of the plan; and the lead authority and the person must, subject to subsection (3), comply with any such direction.

(3)   The lead authority or any other person to whom any direction is given under subsection (2) may appeal to the sheriff against the direction on the grounds that it is unreasonable.

(4) The lead authority is to report annually to the Risk Management Authority as to the implementation of the plan.

(5) Where there has been, or there is likely to be, a significant change in the circumstances of the offender, the lead authority is to review the plan.

(6) Where a review has been carried out under subsection (5), and the lead authority considers that the plan for the time being in force is, or is likely to become, unsuitable, either—

(a) the lead authority is to prepare an amended plan; or

(b) if it is not appropriate for it to continue as lead authority, a different lead authority (determined in accordance with section 7) is to prepare an amended plan,

within such period as the Risk Management Authority may reasonably require.

(7) Sections 6(3) and (4), 8(2) to (7) and this section apply to the preparation of an amended plan under subsection (6) as they do to the preparation of a plan under sections 6 to 8 but as if, in subsection (6)(b) of section 8, the reference to subsection (1) of that section were a reference to subsection (6).

10 Grants to local authorities in connection with risk management plans

(1) The Scottish Ministers may make to any local authority grants of such amount, and subject to such conditions, as they may determine in respect of expenditure incurred by the authority in preparing and implementing any risk management plan.

(2) Before making any such grant, the Scottish Ministers must consult such local authorities and such other persons as they consider appropriate.

11 Accreditation, education and training

(1) The Scottish Ministers may by order make a scheme of accreditation as to—

(a) any manner of assessing and minimising risk (being accreditation in recognition of the effectiveness of any methods and practices which may be employed in the assessment and minimisation of risk); and

(b) persons having functions in relation to the assessment and minimisation of risk (being accreditation in recognition of education or training received, or of any expertise relevant to those functions otherwise held or acquired, by them).

(2) The Risk Management Authority—

(a) is to administer any scheme of accreditation made under subsection (1) (including awarding, generally or for any particular purpose, suspending or withdrawing accreditation where it considers that to be appropriate); and

(b) may provide, or secure the provision of, education and training in relation to the assessment and minimisation of risk for any person having functions in that regard.

12 Functions: supplementary

(1) The Risk Management Authority may, subject to subsection (3), do anything it considers necessary or expedient for the purpose of or in connection with the exercise of its functions.

(2)   In particular, the Authority may—

        (a)   acquire and dispose of land;

        (b)   enter into contracts;

        (c)   charge for goods and services;

        (d)   with the consent of the Scottish Ministers, invest and borrow money.

(3)   The Scottish Ministers may for the purpose of or in connection with the exercise of the Risk Management Authority's functions give directions to the Authority; and the Authority is to comply with any such direction.

13   Accounts and annual reports

(1)   The Risk Management Authority is to—

        (a)   keep proper accounts and accounting records;

        (b)   prepare for each financial year (the financial year being the period of 12 months ending with 31st March) an account of its expenditure and receipts; and

        (c)   send the account to the Scottish Ministers,

    and the Scottish Ministers are to send the account to the Auditor General for Scotland for auditing.

(2)   The Authority is, as soon as practicable after the end of each financial year, to prepare a report on its activities during that year and send a copy of the report to the Scottish Ministers.

(3)   The Scottish Ministers are to lay a copy of the report before the Parliament and publish the report.

PART 2

VICTIMS' RIGHTS

14   Victim statements

(1)   This section applies only where proceedings in respect of an offence are to be taken, or are likely to be taken, in a prescribed court or class of court.

(2)   In so far as is reasonably practicable, a natural person against whom a prescribed offence has been (or appears to have been) perpetrated is—

        (a)   after a decision has been taken to bring proceedings in respect of that offence; or

        (b)   if a procurator fiscal so determines, before any such decision has been taken,

    to be afforded an opportunity to make a statement (to be known as a "victim statement") as to the way in which, and degree to which, that offence (or apparent offence) has affected and as the case may be continues to affect, that person; but this subsection is subject to subsection (6).

(3)   Where a person who has made a victim statement by virtue of subsection (2) (or that subsection and subsection (6)) so requests and sentence may yet fall to be imposed in respect of the offence (or apparent offence), that person is to be afforded an opportunity to make a statement supplementary to, or in amplification of, the victim statement.

(4)   A copy of any—

(a) victim statement made; or

(b) statement made by virtue of subsection (3) in relation to a victim statement,

is, if the accused tenders a plea of guilty to, or is found guilty of, the offence in question, to be provided forthwith to the accused by the prosecutor.

(5) A prosecutor must—

(a) in solemn proceedings, when moving for sentence as respects an offence; and

(b) in summary proceedings, when a plea of guilty is tendered in respect of, or the accused is convicted of, an offence,

lay before the court any victim statement which relates (whether in whole or in part) to the offence in question, and the court must in determining sentence have regard to so much of—

(i) that statement; and

(ii) any statement made by virtue of subsection (3) in relation to that statement,

as it considers to be relevant to that offence.

(6) Where—

(a) because a person has died no such opportunity as is mentioned in subsection (2) can be afforded that person then subsections (2) and (3) apply as if the references in them to the person and to how the offence (or apparent offence) affected, or continues to affect, the person—

(i) were references to any or all of the four qualifying persons highest listed in subsection (10) and to how the offence (or apparent offence) affected, or continues to affect, the maker of the statement; and

(ii) without prejudice to sub-paragraph (i), where the person died a child (that is to say not having attained the age of sixteen years), included references to any other person who, immediately before the offence (or apparent offence) was perpetrated, cared for the child (that expression being construed in accordance with the definition of "person who cares for" in section 2(28) of the Regulation of Care (Scotland) Act 2001 (asp 8)) and to how the offence (or apparent offence) affected, or continues to affect, that other person; or

(b) a person who (but for this paragraph and other than by virtue of paragraph (a)) would be afforded such an opportunity as is so mentioned is—

(i) incapable, by reason of mental disorder or inability to communicate, of making a victim statement, subsections (2) and (3) apply as if the person to be afforded an opportunity were not the incapable person but the qualifying person highest listed in subsection (10); or

(ii) a child who has not attained the age of fourteen years, those subsections apply as if the person to be afforded an opportunity were not that person but such other person as is mentioned in paragraph (a)(ii),

and as if the other references in those subsections to a person continued to be to the incapable person or as the case may be to the child.

(7) For the purposes of subsection (6)(b)(i), inability to communicate by reason only of a lack or deficiency in a faculty of communication is to be disregarded if that lack or deficiency can be made good by human or mechanical aid (whether of an interpretative nature or otherwise).

(8) In subsection (6), "qualifying person" means a person whose relationship to the victim is listed in subsection (10), who is neither incapable as mentioned in sub-paragraph (i) of paragraph (b) of subsection (6) nor a child such as is mentioned in sub-paragraph (ii) of that paragraph and who is not a person referred to by subsection (9).

(9) This subsection refers to a person accused of, or reasonably suspected of being the perpetrator of, or of having been implicated in, the offence (or apparent offence) in question.

(10) The list is—

(a) spouse;

(b) cohabitee;

(c) son or daughter or any person in relation to whom the victim has or had parental responsibilities or rights vested by, under or by virtue of the Children (Scotland) Act 1995 (c.36);

(d) father or mother or any person in whom parental responsibilities or rights are or were vested by, under or by virtue of that Act in relation to the victim;

(e) brother or sister;

(f) grandparent;

(g) grandchild;

(h) uncle or aunt;

(i) nephew or niece,

and the elder of any two persons described in any one of paragraphs (a) to (i) is to be taken to be the higher listed person, regardless of sex.

(11) In subsection (10)(b), "cohabitee" means a person, whether or not of the same sex as the victim, who has lived with the victim, as if in a married relationship, for at least six months and was so living immediately before the offence (or apparent offence) was perpetrated.

(12) The Scottish Ministers may by order (either or both)—

(a) amend subsection (6)(b)(ii) by substituting for the age for the time being specified there such other age as they think fit;

(b) amend the list in subsection (10).

15 Prohibition of personal conduct of defence in proofs ordered in relation to victim statements in cases of certain sexual offences

(1) The 1995 Act is amended as follows.

(2) In section 288C(1) (prohibition of personal conduct of defence in cases of certain sexual offences), at the end there is added "or in any proof ordered in relation to a statement made by virtue of subsection (2) (or by virtue of that subsection and subsection (6)) of section 14 of the Criminal Justice (Scotland) Act 2003 (asp 7)".

(3)   In section 288D(2)(a) (appointment by court of solicitor in such cases), at the end there is added "or as the case may be at any proof ordered as is mentioned in section 288C(1) of this Act".

16   Victim's right to receive information concerning release etc. of offender

(1)   Subject to subsection (2), the Scottish Ministers must, unless they consider that there are exceptional circumstances which make it inappropriate to do so, give any natural person against whom a prescribed offence (or, if they so prescribe, any offence) has been perpetrated such information as is described in subsection (3), being information in relation to any person who has been convicted of that offence and sentenced in respect of it—

(a)   to imprisonment or detention for a period of four or more years;

(b)   to life imprisonment or detention for life; or

(c)   under section 205(2) (punishment for murder where convicted person under 18) or 208 (detention of children convicted on indictment) of the 1995 Act, to detention without limit of time,

provided that the person to be given the information wishes to receive it and has so intimated.

(2)   Subsection (1) does not apply where the convicted person is released before attaining the age of sixteen years.

(3)   The information mentioned in subsection (1) is—

(a)   the date on which the convicted person is, under or by virtue of the 1989 Act or the 1993 Act, released (other than by being granted temporary release);

(b)   if the convicted person dies before that date, the date of death;

(c)   that the convicted person has been transferred to a place outwith Scotland;

(d)   that the convicted person has, by virtue of the 1989 Act, become eligible for temporary release; and

(e)   that the convicted person is unlawfully at large from a prison or young offenders institution.

(4)   The Scottish Ministers may by order—

(a)   amend subsection (1)(a) by substituting, for the period for the time being specified there, a different period; or

(b)   amend subsection (3) by adding descriptions of information.

(5)   Where information would fall to be given to a person under subsection (1) but that person—

(a)   has died, that subsection applies as if references in it to the person were to be construed as mentioned in sub-paragraphs (i) and (ii) of paragraph (a) of section 14(6) of this Act; or

(b)   in a case other than is mentioned in paragraph (a)—

(i)   is incapable as mentioned in sub-paragraph (i) of paragraph (b) of the said section 14(6), that subsection applies as if references in it to the person were to be construed as mentioned in that sub-paragraph; or

(ii)   is a child such as is mentioned in sub-paragraph (ii) of the said paragraph (b), that subsection applies as if references in it to the person were to be construed as mentioned in that sub-paragraph,

(taking him to be the person "afforded an opportunity").

(6)   Subsections (7) and (8) to (12) of section 14 apply in relation to subsection (5) as they apply in relation to subsection (6) of that section.

17   Release on licence: right of victim to receive information and make representations

(1)   Subject to subsections (2), (3) and (12), a person entitled to receive information under section 16 of this Act (the "victim") as respects a convicted person must in accordance with this section, before any decision is taken to release the convicted person on licence, be afforded an opportunity to make written representations to the Scottish Ministers as respects such release and as to conditions which might be specified in the licence in question.

(2)   Subsection (1) applies only where the victim wishes to be afforded the opportunity and has so intimated.

(3)   Subsection (1) does not apply where the convicted person has not attained the age of sixteen years by the date on which the case is referred to the Parole Board for Scotland by the Scottish Ministers.

(4)   The Scottish Ministers are to issue guidance as to how representations under subsection (1) should be framed.

(5)   Where it falls to the Board to recommend whether, or direct that, the convicted person be released, the Scottish Ministers must, as soon as practicable after they commence a review of the case for the purposes of referring it to the Board for the Board to consider what recommendation to make or whether to make such a direction, fix a time within which any representations under subsection (1) require to be made to them if they are to be considered by the Board; and they must notify the victim accordingly.

(6)   Whether or not representations are made under subsection (1), in a case to which subsection (5) applies the Board must, subject to subsection (11)—

     (a)   inform the victim as to whether or not it has recommended or directed release;

     (b)   if it has recommended or directed release, inform the victim as to whether it has also recommended that the person released comply with conditions; and

     (c)   inform the victim of the terms of any such conditions which relate to contact with the victim or with members of the victim's family,

and the Board may provide the victim with such other information as it considers appropriate having regard to the circumstances of the case.

(7)   Where subsection (5) does not apply but it falls to that Board to recommend conditions to be included in the licence, the Scottish Ministers are under the same duties as they are under that subsection.

(8)   Whether or not representations are made under subsection (1), in a case to which subsection (7) applies the Board must inform the victim, subject to subsection (11)—

     (a)   as to whether it has recommended that the person released comply with conditions; and

     (b)   as is mentioned in subsection (6)(c).

(9) Where neither subsection (5) nor (7) applies, the Scottish Ministers must fix a time within which any representations under subsection (1) require to be made to them if they are to be considered by them; and they must notify the victim accordingly.

(10) Whether or not representations are made under subsection (1), in a case to which subsection (9) applies the Scottish Ministers must inform the victim, subject to subsection (11)—

(a) as to whether the person released is to comply with conditions; and

(b) as is mentioned in subsection (6)(c).

(11) Subsections (6), (8) and (10) apply only where the victim has intimated a desire to receive the information in question.

(12) This section does not apply—

(a) as respects release under section 3 of the 1993 Act (release on compassionate grounds); or

(b) where the entitlement mentioned in subsection (1) arises by virtue of section 16(4)(a).

18 Disclosure of certain information relating to victims of crime

(1) Where it appears to a constable that an offence has been perpetrated against a natural person the constable may, with the person's consent, disclose to a prescribed body (being a body which appears to the Scottish Ministers to provide counselling or other support to those who have been victims of crime), with a view to its providing such counselling or support to the person, any or all of the following information—

(a) the person's—

(i) name;

(ii) address;

(iii) telephone number;

(iv) e-mail address;

(v) age;

(b) such information regarding the offence (or apparent offence) as the constable considers appropriate provided that the information does not include such information in relation to the alleged perpetrator as is mentioned in sub-paragraphs (i) to (v) of paragraph (a) (though it may include information as to whether the case is one likely to be disposed of by a children's hearing).

(2) Where the person against whom the offence was perpetrated has died, subsection (1) shall be construed as if it relates not to that person but to any one or more of—

(a) the qualifying persons (as defined in subsection (8) of section 14); and

(b) where the circumstances are as mentioned in sub-paragraph (ii) of subsection (6)(a) of that section, any such other person as is mentioned in that sub-paragraph,

who the constable considers would derive benefit from the counselling or support in question.

PART 3

SEXUAL OFFENCES ETC.

19 Amendments in relation to certain serious and sexual offences

(1) In the Civic Government (Scotland) Act 1982 (c.45)—

  (a) in section 52 (indecent photographs etc. of children), in subsection (3)(b) for the words "3 years" there is substituted "10 years";

  (b) in section 52A (possession of indecent photographs of children), in subsection (3) the existing words from "on summary" to the end become paragraph (a), and after that paragraph there is inserted—

    "(b) on conviction on indictment of such an offence to imprisonment for a period not exceeding 5 years or to a fine or to both.".

(2) In the Criminal Law (Consolidation) (Scotland) Act 1995 (c.39)—

  (a) in section 8 (abduction and unlawful detention), subsections (1) and (2) are repealed;

  (b) section 15 (defence to charge of indecent assault) is repealed;

  (c) in section 16B (commission of certain sexual acts outside the United Kingdom), after subsection (6) there is inserted—

  "(6A) A person may be proceeded against, indicted, tried and punished for any offence to which this section applies—

    (a) in any sheriff court district in Scotland in which he is apprehended or is in custody; or

    (b) in such sheriff court district as the Lord Advocate may determine,

  as if the offence had been committed in that district; and the offence shall, for all purposes incidental to or consequential on trial or punishment, be deemed to have been committed in that district.

  (6B) In subsection (6A) above, "sheriff court district" shall be construed in accordance with section 307(1) (interpretation) of the Criminal Procedure (Scotland) Act 1995 (c.46).".

(3) In the Crime and Punishment (Scotland) Act 1997 (c.48), section 1 (imprisonment for life on further conviction for certain offences) is repealed.

20 Extended sentences

After section 210A of the 1995 Act (extended sentences for sexual or violent offenders) there is inserted—

"210AA Extended sentences for certain other offenders

  Where a person is convicted on indictment of abduction but the offence is other than is mentioned in paragraph (iii) of the definition of "sexual offence" in subsection (10) of section 210A of this Act, that section shall apply in relation to the person as it applies in relation to a person so convicted of a violent offence.".

21   Sexual and certain other offences: reports

(1)   This section applies to any case where a person is convicted of—

    (a)   a sexual offence (as defined in section 210A(10) of the 1995 Act); or

    (b)   an offence the nature and circumstances of which disclose, in the opinion of the court, that there was a significant sexual aspect to the person's behaviour in committing it.

(2)   In a case to which this section applies, the court must, before passing sentence—

    (a)   obtain from a relevant officer a report concerning the person's circumstances and character; and

    (b)   if the conviction is on indictment, obtain from a chartered clinical psychologist or chartered forensic psychologist (that is to say from a person for the time being so described in the British Psychological Society's Register of Chartered Psychologists) a psychological assessment of the person,

and it must also take into account any information before it concerning the person's physical and mental condition.

(3)   The Scottish Ministers may by order amend paragraph (b) of subsection (2) by adding, to the persons for the time being specified there as persons from one of whom a psychological assessment is to be obtained, such description of psychologist as they think fit.

(4)   Where in a case to which this section applies the person is tried, the presiding judge is, as soon as is reasonably practicable, to prepare a report in writing, in such form as may be prescribed by Act of Adjournal—

    (a)   as to the facts established by the evidence; and

    (b)   containing such other information as the judge considers appropriate.

(5)   Where a case to which this section applies does not proceed to trial (or does not proceed to trial as respects part of the complaint or indictment) because a plea of guilty to the complaint, indictment or part in question is accepted by the prosecutor, the narration by the prosecutor, at the diet at which the plea is tendered, of the facts of the case is to be recorded by means of shorthand notes or by mechanical means as is anything said by or on behalf of the person in relation to those facts.

(6)   Subsections (2) to (4) of section 93 of the 1995 Act (certification etc. of notes or record) shall apply in relation to a record made under subsection (5) as they apply in relation to one made under subsection (1) of that section.

(7)   The Scottish Ministers may by order amend subsections (5) and (6) so as to provide for a record so made to be made by such other means as they think fit.

(8)   A copy of any report prepared under subsection (4) or a transcript of any record made under subsection (5) is to be sent to—

    (a)   the officer from whom a report is sought under paragraph (a) of subsection (2) when written intimation of the requirement for the report is first given to that officer; and

    (b)   any psychologist from whom an assessment is sought under paragraph (b) of that subsection when such intimation of the requirement for that assessment is first given to that psychologist.

(9)   In relation to a case to which this section applies, subsection (3) of section 201 of the 1995 Act (limitation as respects power of court to adjourn case before sentence) shall have effect as if for the words—

  (a)   "three weeks" in paragraph (a); and

  (b)   "four weeks" in paragraph (b),

there were in each case substituted "six weeks".

(10)   In that subsection, at the beginning, there is inserted "Subject to section 21(9) of the Criminal Justice (Scotland) Act 2003 (asp 7),".

(11)   In subsection (2)(a), "relevant officer" means an officer—

  (a)   of the local authority for the area within which the convicted person resides; and

  (b)   employed by them in the discharge of their functions under section 27(1) (supervision and care of persons put on probation or released from prison etc.) or 27AA (advice, guidance and assistance to persons arrested or on whom sentence deferred) of the Social Work (Scotland) Act 1968 (c.49).

22   Traffic in prostitution etc.

(1)   A person commits an offence who arranges or facilitates—

  (a)   the arrival in the United Kingdom of, or travel there (whether or not following such arrival) by, an individual and—

    (i)   intends to exercise control over prostitution by the individual or to involve the individual in the making or production of obscene or indecent material; or

    (ii)   believes that another person is likely to exercise such control or so to involve the individual,

  there or elsewhere; or

  (b)   the departure from there of an individual and—

    (i)   intends to exercise such control or so to involve the individual; or

    (ii)   believes that another person is likely to exercise such control or so to involve the individual,

  outwith the United Kingdom.

(2)   For the purposes of subsection (1), a person exercises control over prostitution by an individual if the person exercises control, direction or influence over the prostitute's movements in a way which shows that the person is aiding, abetting or compelling the prostitution.

(3)   A person guilty of an offence under this section is liable—

  (a)   on conviction on indictment, to imprisonment for a term not exceeding fourteen years, to a fine or to both; or

  (b)   on summary conviction, to imprisonment for a term not exceeding six months, to a fine not exceeding the statutory maximum or to both.

(4)   Subsection (1) applies to anything done—

  (a)   in the United Kingdom; or

(b) outwith the United Kingdom—

    (i)   by an individual to whom subsection (6) applies; or

    (ii) by a body incorporated under the law of a part of the United Kingdom.

(5)   If an offence under this section is committed outwith the United Kingdom, proceedings may be taken in any place in Scotland; and the offence may for incidental purposes be treated as having been committed in that place.

(6)   This subsection applies to—

    (a)   a British citizen;

    (b)   a British overseas territories citizen;

    (c)   a British National (Overseas);

    (d)   a British Overseas citizen;

    (e)   a person who is a British subject under the British Nationality Act 1981 (c.61); and

    (f)   a British protected person within the meaning of that Act.

(7)   In this section, "material" has the same meaning as in section 51 of the Civic Government (Scotland) Act 1982 (c.45) and includes a pseudo-photograph within the meaning of section 52 of that Act, a copy of a pseudo-photograph and data stored on a computer disc or by any other electronic means which is capable of conversion into a photograph or pseudo-photograph.

PART 4

PRISONERS ETC.

Custody and temporary detention

23   Remand and committal of children and young persons

(1)   In section 19(1)(b) of the 1989 Act (construction of expression "young offenders institution"), at the end there is added "and in which certain such persons as are mentioned in paragraph (a) above may be kept".

(2)   In section 40 of that Act (persons unlawfully at large), in each of subsections (1) and (2), after the words "a prison" there is inserted "or young offenders institution".

(3)   In subsection (1) of section 51 of the 1995 Act (remand and committal of children and young persons)—

    (a)   in paragraph (a)—

       (i)   the words "subject to paragraph (b) below," are repealed; and

       (ii) for the words "the court shall, instead of committing him to prison," there is substituted "but is not a child to whom paragraph (bb) below applies, the court shall";

    (b)   in paragraph (aa)—

       (i)   for the words "is over 16 years of age and" there is substituted "has attained the age of 16 years and is";

       (ii) the words ", instead of committing him to prison," are repealed; and

(iii) at the end there is added "or may commit him either to prison or to a young offenders institution";

(c) for paragraph (b) there is substituted—

"(b) if he is a person who has attained the age of 16 years and to whom paragraph (aa) above does not apply, then where—

(i) the court has been notified by the Scottish Ministers that a remand centre is available for the reception from that court of persons of his class or description, it shall commit him to a remand centre; or

(ii) the court has not been so notified, it may commit him either to prison or to a young offenders institution;

(bb) if he is a child who is under 16 years of age but has attained the age of 14 years and is certified by the court to be unruly or depraved, then where—

(i) the court has been so notified as is mentioned in paragraph (b)(i) above, it shall commit him to a remand centre; or

(ii) the court has not been so notified, it may commit him either to prison or to a young offenders institution.".

(4) In subsection (2) of that section the words "or to a remand centre", "or centre" and "or in the centre" are repealed.

(5) After subsection (2) of that section there is inserted—

"(2A) Subject to subsection (4) below, where any person is committed to a remand centre under any provision of this Act, he shall be detained in a remand centre for the period for which he is committed or until he is liberated in due course of law.".

(6) In subsection (3)(b) of that section, for the words "to a prison" there is substituted "either to prison or to a young offenders institution".

(7) In subsection (4) of that section—

(a) for the words "to prison or to a remand centre under this section" there is substituted "under this section to prison, to a young offenders institution or to a remand centre"; and

(b) after the words "or a" there is inserted "young offenders institution or".

(8) At the end of that section there is added—

"(5) Where by virtue of subsection (1)(aa), (b)(ii), (bb)(ii) or (3)(b) of this section a person is committed either to prison or to a young offenders institution, the warrant issued by the court is warrant also, without further application to the court in that regard, for committal to whichever of the two the court does not specify.".

24   Legal custody

(1) In section 13 of the 1989 Act (legal custody of prisoners)—

(a) for the words "A person shall be deemed to be" there is substituted "Without prejudice to section 295 of the Criminal Procedure (Scotland) Act 1995 (c.46) (legal custody of persons generally), a prisoner is"; and

    (b) in paragraph (b), at the end there is added ", a constable ("constable" having the same meaning as it has, by virtue of paragraph 17(1) and (2) of Schedule 1 to the Crime (Sentences) Act 1997 (c.43), in section 40(1) of this Act) or a police custody and security officer".

(2)   In section 295 of the 1995 Act (legal custody of persons generally)—

    (a) at the beginning there is inserted "Without prejudice to section 13 of the Prisons (Scotland) Act 1989 (c.45) (legal custody of prisoners),";

    (b) for the word "shall" there is substituted "is"; and

    (c) the words "be deemed to be" are repealed.

25   **Temporary detention of person being returned to prison in England and Wales etc.**

After section 40A of the1989 Act there is inserted—

    "40B   **Temporary detention of person being returned to prison in England and Wales etc.**

Any person absent, otherwise than with lawful authority, from a place outwith Scotland, being a place to which, by virtue of paragraph 17 of Schedule 1 to the Crime (Sentences) Act 1997 (c.43) (application throughout United Kingdom and Channel Islands of certain enactments relating to the arrest and return of prisoners etc.), he may be taken, may, until the arrangements to take him can be made, be detained in a prison or young offenders institution in Scotland.".

Consecutive sentences

26   **Consecutive sentences: life prisoners etc.**

(1)   After section 204A of the 1995 Act (which restricts the ability of a court to impose consecutive sentences in the case of prisoners released on licence etc.), there is inserted—

    "204B   **Consecutive sentences: life prisoners etc.**

    (1) This section applies in respect of sentencing for offences committed after the coming into force of this section.

    (2) Where, in solemn proceedings, the court sentences a person to imprisonment or other detention, the court may—

        (a) if the person is serving or is liable to serve the punishment part of a previous sentence, frame the sentence to take effect on the day after that part of that sentence is or would be due to expire; or

        (b) if the person is serving or is liable to serve the punishment parts of two or more previous sentences, frame the sentence to take effect on the day after the later or (as the case may be) latest expiring of those parts is or would be due to expire.

    (3) Where, in such proceedings, it falls to the court to sentence a person who is subject to a previous sentence in respect of which a punishment part requires to be (but has not been) specified, the court shall not sentence the person until such time as the part is either specified or no longer requires to be specified.

(4)   Where the court sentences a person to a sentence of imprisonment or other detention for life, for an indeterminate period or without limit of time, the court may, if the person is serving or is liable to serve for any offence—

(a)   a previous sentence of imprisonment or other detention the term of which is not treated as part of a single term under section 27(5) of the 1993 Act; or

(b)   two or more previous sentences of imprisonment or other detention the terms of which are treated as a single term under that section of that Act,

frame the sentence to take effect on the day after the person would (but for the sentence so framed and disregarding any subsequent sentence) be entitled to be released under the provisions referred to in section 204A of this Act as respects the sentence or sentences.

(5)   Subsection (4)(a) above shall not apply where the sentence is a sentence from which he has been released at any time under the provisions referred to in section 204A of this Act.

(6)   In this section, any reference to a punishment part of a sentence shall be construed by reference to—

(a)   the punishment part of the sentence as is specified in an order mentioned in section 2(2) of the 1993 Act; or

(b)   any part of the sentence which has effect, by virtue of section 10 of the 1993 Act or the schedule to the Convention Rights (Compliance) (Scotland) Act 2001 (asp 7), as if it were the punishment part so specified,

and "the 1993 Act" means the Prisoners and Criminal Proceedings (Scotland) Act 1993 (c.9).

(7)   This section is without prejudice to any other power under any enactment or rule of law as respects sentencing.".

(2)   Section 167 of that Act (forms of finding and sentence) is amended as follows—

(a)   in subsection (7) after the words "any previous sentence" there is inserted "for a term"; and

(b)   after that subsection, there is inserted—

"(7A)   Where the court imposes a sentence as mentioned in paragraph (a) of subsection (7) above for an offence committed after the coming into force of this subsection, the court may—

(a)   if the person is serving or is liable to serve the punishment part of a previous sentence, frame the sentence to take effect on the day after that part of that sentence is or would be due to expire; or

(b)   if the person is serving or is liable to serve the punishment parts of two or more previous sentences, frame the sentence to take effect on the day after the later or (as the case may be) latest expiring of those parts is or would be due to expire.

(7B)   Where it falls to the court to sentence a person who is subject to a previous sentence in respect of which a punishment part requires to be (but has not been) specified, the court shall not sentence the person until such time as the part is either specified or no longer requires to be specified.

(7C) In subsections (7A) and (7B) above, any reference to a punishment part of a sentence shall be construed by reference to—

    (a) the punishment part of the sentence as is specified in an order mentioned in section 2(2) of the 1993 Act; or

    (b) any part of the sentence which has effect, by virtue of section 10 of the 1993 Act or the schedule to the Convention Rights (Compliance) (Scotland) Act 2001 (asp 7), as if it were the punishment part so specified,

and "the 1993 Act" means the Prisoners and Criminal Proceedings (Scotland) Act 1993 (c.9).".

Release of prisoners

27   **Release on licence etc. under 1989 Act**

(1) The 1989 Act (certain provisions of which, notwithstanding their repeal by the 1993 Act, continue to apply to prisoners sentenced before 1st October 1993 by virtue of section 47(2) of, and paragraph 2(1) of Schedule 6 to, that Act) is amended for the purposes of the existing provisions, within the meaning of that Schedule, as follows.

(2) In section 22 (which, among other things, enables the Scottish Ministers to release on licence certain prisoners if recommended to do so by the Parole Board and, by virtue of subsection (1A) of that section, requires them to release certain other prisoners if there is such a recommendation)—

    (a) in subsection (1), for the word "may" there is substituted "shall";

    (b) subsection (1A) is repealed; and

    (c) in subsection (7)—

        (i) the words "and by virtue of subsection (1A) above such release is then mandatory"; and

        (ii) the words from "; and in any other case" to the end,

    are repealed.

28   **Release on licence etc. under 1993 Act**

(1) The 1993 Act (which applies to prisoners sentenced on or after 1st October 1993 and to some prisoners sentenced before that date) is amended as follows.

(2) In section 1(3) (which enables the Scottish Ministers to release on licence certain prisoners if recommended to do so by the Parole Board and, by virtue of section 20(3)(a), requires them to release certain other prisoners if there is such a recommendation), for the word "may" there is substituted—

    "(a) shall, except in the case mentioned in paragraph (b) below; or

    (b) may, in the case of a prisoner who is liable to removal from the United Kingdom (within the meaning of section 9 of this Act),".

(3) In section 12 (which enables the Scottish Ministers to insert, vary or cancel conditions in licences and, in certain cases, to do so in accordance with the recommendations of the Parole Board), for subsections (3) and (4) there is substituted—

"(3)   The Scottish Ministers may under subsection (1) above include on release and from time to time insert, vary or cancel a condition in a licence granted under this Part of this Act; but—

(a) in the case of a long-term or life prisoner released by the Scottish Ministers under subsection (1) of section 3 of this Act without consulting the Parole Board, no licence condition shall be inserted, varied or cancelled subsequent to the release except in accordance with the recommendations of the Parole Board; and

(b) in the case of any other long-term or life prisoner, no licence condition shall be included on release, or subsequently inserted, varied or cancelled except in accordance with such recommendations.".

(4)   Section 20(3) (which provides power to modify the effect of section 1(3) in relation to certain classes of case) is repealed.

29   Release on licence: life prisoners

(1)   The 1993 Act is amended as follows.

(2)   In section 2 (which provides, among other things, for consideration by the Parole Board of whether a life prisoner should be released on licence)—

(a) in subsection (5A)(b), after the word "being" there is inserted ", subject to subsections (5AB) to (5AD) below,";

(b) after that subsection there is inserted—

"(5AB) Where a reference has been made to the Parole Board under any of the provisions mentioned in subsection (5A) above and the prisoner receives another sentence of imprisonment (whether for life or for a term) before a date has been fixed for considering his case, the Board shall, if he would not be eligible for release from the other sentence on the date which would (apart from this subsection) have been fixed for considering his case, fix a date (other than that date) for considering his case.

(5AC) Where, at any time after such a reference has been made—

(a) a date has been fixed for considering the prisoner's case; or

(b) following the disposal of the reference, a date has been fixed under subsection (5A)(b) above,

and, before that date, the prisoner receives any other sentence of imprisonment (whether for life or for a term), the Board shall, if he would not be eligible for release from any such other sentence on that date, fix a different date for considering his case (and where he receives any further sentence of imprisonment from which he would not be eligible for release on that different date, the Board shall fix a further different date).

(5AD) Any date fixed under subsection (5AB) or (5AC) above shall—

(a) be—

(i) the date on which the prisoner would be eligible to be released, or considered for release, from all such other sentences (subject to any change to the date on which he would be so eligible); or

(ii) a date as soon as practicable after that date; and

      (b) replace any date previously fixed for considering the prisoner's case.";

(c) in—

    (i) subsection (5B); and

    (ii) subsection (5C),

after the words "subsection (5A)(b)" there is in each case inserted ", (5AB) or (5AC)";

(d) for subsection (7) there is substituted—

"(7) No requirement shall be made under subsection (6) above by a life prisoner who is also serving or liable to serve a sentence of imprisonment for a term, before he has served the appropriate part of the term.

(7A) The appropriate part of the term is—

    (a) one half, where the term is—

      (i) less than 4 years; or

      (ii) 4 years or more and is imposed by a sentence of imprisonment on conviction of an offence; or

    (b) two thirds, where the term is 4 years or more and is a term of imprisonment or detention mentioned in section 5(1)(a) or (b) of this Act.

(7B) Section 5(1) of this Act, in so far as relating to the construction of references to sentences of imprisonment, does not apply to subsection (7A)(b) above."; and

(e) in subsection (9), after the word "serving" there is inserted "or is liable to serve".

(3) In section 5(1) (which applies, with modification, the provisions of the 1993 Act concerning persons sentenced to imprisonment, or detention, on conviction of an offence to persons on whom imprisonment, or detention, has been imposed for non-payment of fine or for contempt of court), for the words "section 1(8)" there is substituted "sections 1(8) and 2(7B)".

30   Release on licence: certain consecutive sentences

In section 1A (application to persons serving more than one sentence) of the 1993 Act—

(a) the existing words become subsection (1); and

(b) after that subsection there is added—

"(2) Where a prisoner who is serving any term of imprisonment receives a sentence of imprisonment or other detention for life, for an indeterminate period or without limit of time which is to take effect on the day after he would (but for the sentence so received) be entitled to be released from the term, nothing in this Part of this Act shall require—

    (a) the Scottish Ministers to release him in respect of any such term unless and until they are required to release him in respect of the sentence so received; or

(b) the Scottish Ministers or the Parole Board to consider his release in respect of any such term unless and until the Scottish Ministers are or the Parole Board is required to consider his release, or the Scottish Ministers are required to release him, in respect of the sentence so received.".

31   Release: prisoners serving extended sentences

In section 3A (re-release of prisoners serving extended sentences) of the 1993 Act—

(a) in subsection (1)—

(i)   at the beginning there is inserted "Subject to subsection (1A) below,"; and

(ii)   for the words "who has been recalled to prison under section 17(1)" there is substituted "and in respect of whom a licence has been revoked under section 17(1) to (1B)";

(b) after subsection (1) there is inserted—

"(1A) This section does not apply to such a prisoner if he has, in addition to the sentence in relation to which his recall to prison applies, been sentenced to imprisonment for life and has not been released from that sentence.";

(c) in subsection (2), in paragraph (a), for the words "disposal of that referral" there is substituted "Board's disposal of his case";

(d) after that subsection there is inserted—

"(2A) Where—

(a) a prisoner's case has been referred to the Parole Board under this section or section 17(3) of this Act; and

(b) the prisoner receives another sentence of imprisonment before the Board has considered his case,

the Board shall not consider his case unless there is a further referral of his case to the Board under this section.

(2B) A case which, by virtue of subsection (2A) above, is not considered by the Parole Board shall not, for the purposes of subsection (2)(a) above, be treated as having been disposed of."; and

(e) in subsection (3)—

(i)   for the word "sentence" in the second place where it appears there is substituted "term"; and

(ii)   for the words "has served one half of" there is substituted "would be eligible to be released, or considered for release, from".

32   Release etc. under 1993 Act of prisoner serving consecutive or concurrent offence and non-offence terms

(1) The 1993 Act is amended as follows.

(2) In section 27 (interpretation of Part I), after subsection (4) there is inserted—

"(4A) For the purposes of this Part of this Act, a term of imprisonment or detention—

(a) is wholly concurrent with another such term (or other such terms) if—

(i)   it is imposed on the same date as that other term (or terms); and

(ii) it expires on the same date as that other term (or terms); and

(b) is partly concurrent with another such term (or other such terms) if—

(i) it is imposed on the same date as, and expires on a different date from, that other term (or terms); or

(ii) it is imposed on a different date from, but before the expiry of, that other term (or terms).".

(3) In Schedule 1 (which makes special provision as respects eligibility for early release from consecutive or wholly or partly concurrent offence and non-offence terms of imprisonment or detention)—

(a) for paragraph 2 (consecutive terms) there is substituted—

"2 (1) Where his offence term and his non-offence term are consecutive, whichever term follows the other shall be taken as beginning on the day after he is released as respects the other term.

(2) For the purposes of sub-paragraph (1) above, where his offence term and his non-offence term are imposed on the same date, his non-offence term shall be taken to follow his offence term.

Concurrent terms of imprisonment

2A Where his offence term and his non-offence term are wholly or partly concurrent, section 1(1) to (3) of this Act (so far as relevant to the term in question and whether or not modified by section 5(2) of this Act or as read with section 220 of the 1995 Act (reduction of term in certain circumstances)) shall apply separately to each term (that is to say, in particular, he may be released as respects one of the terms even if he is not for the time being eligible for release as respects the other term)."; and

(b) paragraphs 3 (wholly concurrent terms) and 4 (partly concurrent terms) are repealed.

33   Prisoners repatriated to Scotland

(1) In the Repatriation of Prisoners Act 1984 (c.47)—

(a) in subsection (9) of section 3 (transfer into the United Kingdom), the words "or section 10 of the Prisoners and Criminal Proceedings (Scotland) Act 1993" and "or, as the case may be, Scotland" are repealed; and

(b) in the Schedule (operation of certain enactments in relation to the prisoner)—

(i) for paragraph 2 there is substituted—

"*Early release*

2 (1) In determining, for the purposes of sections 1(1) to (3), 2(2) and (7) and 7(1) of the Prisoners and Criminal Proceedings (Scotland) Act 1993 (c.9), in their application to prisoners repatriated to Scotland (eligibility for early release from a sentence), whether the prisoner has at any time served a particular proportion or part of the sentence, the sentence shall, subject to sub-paragraph (2) below, be deemed to begin with the day on which the relevant provisions take effect.

(2)   If the warrant specifies a period to be taken into account for the purposes of section 1(3) or 2(2) or (7) of that Act (eligibility of long-term and life prisoners as respects release on licence)—

(a)   the amount of time the prisoner has served; and

(b)   where the sentence is a determinate one, the sentence,

shall, so far only as the question whether he has served any particular proportion or part of the sentence is concerned, be deemed to be increased by that period.

(3)   The question whether the prisoner is a short-term or a long-term prisoner for the purposes of any of the sections mentioned in sub-paragraph (1) above shall be determined by reference to the length of the sentence imposed in the country or territory from which he is transferred.

(4)   For the purposes of Schedule 6 to that Act, a prisoner's sentence shall be deemed to have been imposed on the day on which the relevant provisions take effect.

(5)   In this paragraph, "sentence", except in sub-paragraph (3) above, means the provision included in the warrant which is equivalent to a sentence."; and

(ii)   paragraph 3 is repealed.

(2)   Subsection (1)(b)(i) applies in relation to prisoners repatriated to Scotland on or after the coming into force of this section any of whose sentences in the country or territory from which they are transferred were imposed on or after 1st October 1993.

(3)   In paragraph 1 of Schedule 6 (transitional provisions and savings) to the 1993 Act, in the definition of "new provisions", after the words "1997" there is inserted "and section 33 of the Criminal Justice (Scotland) Act 2003 (asp 7)".

(4)   In paragraph 7 of Schedule 2 (repatriation of prisoners to the British Islands) to the Crime (Sentences) Act 1997 (c.43), in sub-paragraph (1), for the words from "for" to the end there is substituted "but before the commencement of section 33 of the Criminal Justice (Scotland) Act 2003 (asp 7)".

34   Suspension of conditions and revocation of licences under 1989 Act

(1)   The 1989 Act is amended for the purposes of the existing provisions (within the meaning of Schedule 6 to the 1993 Act) as follows.

(2)   In subsection (6) of section 22 (which requires a person released on licence under that section to comply with such conditions as may be specified in the licence), after the word "shall" there is inserted ", subject to section 22A below,".

(3)   After that section there is inserted—

"22A   Suspension of licence conditions

(1)   Where a prisoner, who has been released on licence under section 22 of this Act as respects a sentence of imprisonment—

(a)   continues, by virtue of any enactment or rule of law, to be detained in prison notwithstanding such release; or

(b)   is, by virtue of any enactment or rule of law, detained in prison subsequent to the date of such release but while the licence remains in force, the conditions in the licence, other than those mentioned in subsection (3) below, shall by virtue of such detention be suspended.

(2)   The suspension of the conditions shall have effect for so long as—

    (a)   the prisoner is so detained; and

    (b)   the licence remains in force.

(3)   The conditions are any conditions, however expressed, requiring the prisoner—

    (a)   to be of good behaviour and to keep the peace; or

    (b)   not to contact a named person or class of persons (or not to do so unless with the approval of a person specified in the licence by virtue of section 22(7) of this Act).

(4)   The Scottish Ministers may by order amend subsection (3) above by—

    (a)   adding to the conditions mentioned in that subsection such other conditions as they consider appropriate; or

    (b)   cancelling or varying a condition for the time being mentioned in that subsection.".

(4)   In section 28 (which, among other things, enables the Scottish Ministers to revoke the licence of, and recall to prison, certain prisoners if recommended to do so by the Parole Board and, by virtue of subsection (1A) of that section, requires them to revoke the licence of and recall to prison certain other prisoners if there is such a recommendation)—

    (a)   in subsection (1), for the word "may" there is substituted "shall"; and

    (b)   subsection (1A) is repealed.

35   Suspension of licence conditions under 1993 Act

(1)   The 1993 Act is amended as follows.

(2)   In section 12 (which requires a person released on licence under Part I of that Act to comply with the conditions specified in the licence), in subsection (1), after the word "shall" there is inserted ", subject to section 12A below,".

(3)   After that section there is inserted—

"12A   Suspension of licence conditions

(1)   Where a prisoner, who has been released on licence under this Part of this Act as respects a sentence of imprisonment—

    (a)   continues, by virtue of any enactment or rule of law, to be detained in prison notwithstanding such release; or

    (b)   is, by virtue of any enactment or rule of law, detained in prison subsequent to the date of such release but while the licence remains in force,

the conditions in the licence, other than those mentioned in subsection (3) below, shall by virtue of such detention be suspended.

(2)   The suspension of the conditions shall have effect for so long as—

    (a)   the prisoner is so detained; and

(b)   the licence remains in force.

(3)   The conditions are any conditions, however expressed, requiring the prisoner—

  (a)   to be of good behaviour and to keep the peace; or

  (b)   not to contact a named person or class of persons (or not to do so unless with the approval of the person specified in the licence by virtue of section 12(2)(a) of this Act).

(4)   The Scottish Ministers may by order amend subsection (3) above by—

  (a)   adding to the conditions mentioned in that subsection such other condition as they consider appropriate; or

  (b)   cancelling or varying a condition for the time being mentioned in that subsection.

12B   Certain licences to be replaced by one

(1)   Subsection (2) below applies where a prisoner—

  (a)   has been released on licence under this Part of this Act or under the 1989 Act as respects any sentence of imprisonment ("the original sentence"); and

  (b)   while so released, receives another sentence of imprisonment (whether for life or for a term) ("the subsequent sentence"),

and the licence as respects the original sentence has not been revoked.

(2)   Where—

  (a)   this subsection applies; and

  (b)   the prisoner is to be released on licence under this Part of this Act as respects the subsequent sentence,

he shall instead be released on a single licence under this Part of this Act as respects both the original sentence and the subsequent sentence.

(3)   The single licence—

  (a)   shall have effect in place of—

      (i)   the licence as respects the original sentence; and

      (ii)   any licence on which the prisoner would, apart from this section, be released as respects the subsequent sentence;

  (b)   shall be subject to such conditions as were in the licence as respects the original sentence immediately before that licence was replaced by the single licence; and

  (c)   shall (unless revoked) remain in force for so long as any licence as respects the original sentence or as respects the subsequent sentence would, apart from this section (and if not revoked), have remained in force.".

36   Revocation of licences under 1993 Act

(1)   The 1993 Act is amended as follows.

(2)   In section 5(2) (fine defaulters and persons in contempt of court), for the words from "both" to "17(1)" there is substituted "released on licence under section 3 of this Act and, subsequently, the licence is revoked under section 17(1), (1A) or (1B)".

(3)   In section 16(7) (which provides that a court order that a long-term or short-term prisoner released on licence be returned to prison has the effect of automatically revoking the licence), paragraph (a), and the word "and" immediately following that paragraph, are repealed.

(4)   In section 17 (which enables the Scottish Ministers to revoke the licence of, and recall to prison, certain prisoners if recommended to do so by the Parole Board, enables them to do so in certain circumstances without such a recommendation, and requires them to do so as respects certain prisoners if there is such a recommendation), for subsections (1) to (3) there is substituted—

"(1)   Where—

(a)   a long-term prisoner has been released on licence under this Part of this Act and is not detained as mentioned in section 12A(1)(a) or (b) of this Act; or

(b)   a life prisoner has been so released on licence and is not detained as mentioned in section 12A(1)(b) of this Act,

the Scottish Ministers—

(i)   shall, if recommended to do so by the Parole Board; or

(ii)   may, if revocation and recall are, in their opinion, expedient in the public interest and it is not practicable to await such a recommendation,

revoke the licence and recall the prisoner to prison.

(1A)   Where a long-term prisoner or a life prisoner has been released on licence as mentioned in subsection (1) above, but is detained as mentioned in that subsection, the Scottish Ministers—

(a)   shall, if recommended to do so by the Parole Board; or

(b)   may, if revocation is, in their opinion, expedient in the public interest and it is not practicable to await such a recommendation,

revoke the licence.

(1B)   Where a short-term prisoner has been released on licence under section 3(1) of this Act, the Scottish Ministers may, whether or not he is detained as mentioned in section 12A(1)(b) of this Act—

(a)   revoke the licence; and

(b)   where he is not so detained, recall him to prison,

if they are satisfied that his health or circumstances have so changed that his release on licence is no longer justified.

(2)   The Scottish Ministers shall, on the revocation of a person's licence under subsection (1), (1A) or (1B) above, inform that person of the reasons for the revocation.

(3)   The Scottish Ministers shall refer to the Parole Board the case of a person whose licence is revoked under subsection (1), (1A) or (1B) above.".

37   Extended sentences: recall to prison and revocation of licences

(1)   The 1993 Act is amended as follows.

(2)   In section 26A (which applies, with adaptations, the other provisions of Part I of the 1993 Act to prisoners who are subject to an extended sentence), for subsection (9) there is substituted—

> "(9)   In relation to a prisoner subject to an extended sentence, the reference in section 17(5) of this Act to the prisoner being "liable to be detained in pursuance of his sentence" shall be construed as a reference to the prisoner being liable to be detained until the expiry of the extension period.".

38   Special provision in relation to children

(1)   The 1993 Act is amended as follows.

(2)   In section 7 (which among other things enables the Scottish Ministers to release on licence certain children if recommended to do so by the Parole Board, and which provides that a court order that a child released on licence be returned to detention has the effect of automatically revoking the licence)—

(a)   in subsection (2), for the word "may" there is substituted "shall";

(b)   subsection (4A) is repealed;

(c)   for subsection (5), there is substituted—

> "(5)   Without prejudice to section 6(1)(b)(ii) of this Act—
>
> > (a)   sections 3, 11(1), 12, 12A, 12B, 17 and 20(2) of this Act apply to children detained under section 208 of the 1995 Act as they apply to long-term prisoners; and
> >
> > (b)   in those sections of this Act, references to prisoners, or to prison, imprisonment or sentences of imprisonment shall be construed, and sections 1A and 27 shall apply, accordingly."; and

(d)   subsection (6) is repealed.

Special provision as regards certain life prisoners

39   Convention rights of certain life prisoners

In the schedule to the Convention Rights (Compliance) (Scotland) Act 2001 (asp 7)—

(a)   in Part 1 (existing life prisoners), after paragraph 7 there is inserted—

> "7A   In the case of a prisoner to whom paragraph 6 above applies, Part 1 of the 1993 Act as amended by this Act shall apply as if the part of the prisoner's sentence specified in the certificate mentioned in paragraph 1(b) above were a punishment part specified under section 2(2) of the 1993 Act as amended by this Act."; and

(b)   in Part 4 (transferred life prisoners)—

(i)   after paragraph 49 there is inserted—

> "49A   This Part of this schedule also applies to—
>
> > (a)   any life prisoner who was transferred—

            (i)   on or after the coming into force of section 10 of the 1993 Act; and

            (ii)   before the relevant date,

and to whom, by virtue of the Crime and Punishment (Scotland) Act 1997 (c.48), subsections (2) and (3) of that section applied subsequent to the prisoner's transfer; and

     (b)   any other life prisoner who was—

            (i)   transferred to Scotland before the coming into effect of section 10 of the 1993 Act; and

            (ii)   as at the relevant date, a life prisoner such as is mentioned in any of sub-paragraphs (a) to (c) of paragraph 49 above (the references in those sub-paragraphs to that section being construed as references to that section as it had effect on that date).";

     (ii)   in paragraph 50, after the word "49" there is inserted "or 49A";

     (iii) in paragraph 53, after the word "applies" there is inserted ", to whom sub-paragraph (a) of paragraph 49A above applies (whether or not paragraph 49(b) above also applies to the prisoner) or to whom sub-paragraph (b) of paragraph 49A above applies (in so far as that sub-paragraph relates to paragraph 49(c) above)";

     (iv) in paragraph 54, for the words from "to" in the first place where it occurs to "applies" there is substituted "such as is mentioned in paragraph 52 or 53 above"; and

     (v)   for paragraph 67 there is substituted—

"67   In the case of a prisoner to whom paragraph 53 above applies, Part 1 of the 1993 Act (except subsection (9) of section 2) as amended by this Act shall apply as if—

     (a)   the prisoner were a life prisoner within the meaning of subsection (1) of that section; and

     (b)   the part of the prisoner's sentence specified in the certificate referred to in sub-paragraph (c) of paragraph 57 above were a punishment part specified under subsection (2) of that section.".

Monitoring on release

40   Remote monitoring of released prisoners

  (1)   This section applies where a person is released on licence under—

     (a)   section 22 of the 1989 Act (persons sentenced before 1st October 1993); or

     (b)   Part I of the 1993 Act (persons sentenced on or after that date),

but in the case of a person released under that Part by virtue of section 7(5) of the 1993 Act (application of certain provisions to children detained in solemn proceedings) only if, at release, that person has attained the age of sixteen years.

  (2)   Conditions which may be specified in the licence include conditions for securing the remote monitoring of the person's—

     (a)   compliance with any other condition so specified;

(b) whereabouts (other than for the purposes of paragraph (a)).

(3) Where the Scottish Ministers specify such conditions in the licence they must designate in it a person who is to be responsible for the monitoring and must, as soon as practicable after they do so, send that person a copy of the conditions so specified together with such information as they consider requisite to the fulfilment of the responsibility.

(4) Subject to subsection (5), the designated person's responsibility—

(a) commences on that person's receipt of the copy so sent;

(b) is suspended during any period in which the conditions for securing the monitoring are suspended; and

(c) ends when those conditions are cancelled or the licence is revoked or otherwise ceases to be in force.

(5) The Scottish Ministers may from time to time designate a person who, in place of the person designated under subsection (3) (or last designated under this subsection), is to be responsible for the monitoring; and on the Scottish Ministers amending the licence in respect of the new designation, that subsection and subsection (4) apply in relation to the person designated under this subsection as they apply in relation to the person replaced.

(6) If a designation under subsection (5) is made, the Scottish Ministers must, in so far as it is practicable to do so, notify the person replaced accordingly.

(7) Section 245C of the 1995 Act (contractual and other arrangements for, and devices which may be used for the purposes of, remote monitoring) applies in relation to the imposition of, and compliance with, conditions specified by virtue of subsection (2) as that section applies in relation to the making of, and compliance with, a restriction of liberty order.

(8) A designation under this section is not a licence condition for the purposes of—

(a) section 22(7) of the 1989 Act (requirement for recommendation of Parole Board); or

(b) section 12(3)(b) of the 1993 Act (requirement for recommendation of, or consultation with, Parole Board).

Parole Board to have regard to risk management plans

41   Parole Board to have regard to risk management plans

In the 1993 Act, after section 26A, there is inserted—

"26B   Parole Board to have regard to risk management plans

The Parole Board shall, whenever it is considering the case of a person in respect of whom there is a risk management plan, have regard to the plan.".

PART 5

DRUGS COURTS

42   Drugs courts

(1)   It may be prescribed that a court, or class of court, is designated as a "drugs court"; that is to say, as a court especially appropriate to deal with cases involving persons dependent on, or with a propensity to misuse, drugs.

(2)   It may be prescribed that there is to be a drugs court within (either or both)—

    (a)   a sheriffdom or sheriff court district, in which case the sheriff principal is, subject to subsection (1), to nominate a court within that sheriffdom or as the case may be sheriff court district;

    (b)   a commission area, in which case the clerk of the district court is, subject to that subsection, to nominate a district court constituted by a stipendiary magistrate,

to be a drugs court.

(3)   Any designation under subsection (1) or nomination under subsection (2) is without prejudice to the powers and jurisdiction of any court; but only a drugs court is to have the powers provided for in subsection (4), being powers—

    (a)   additional to any other powers the court may have; and

    (b)   exercisable only as respects such persons as the court is satisfied are persons such as are mentioned in subsection (1).

(4)   The powers are, that where an offender has failed to comply with the requirements of a drug treatment and testing order or a probationer with the requirements of a probation order, the court may, subject to subsections (6) and (7), on one, or more than one, occasion—

    (a)   sentence that person to imprisonment, or as the case may be detention, so however that the total of all periods so imposed in respect of the order is not to exceed twenty-eight days (and accordingly any one such period may be less than any minimum sentence which, but for this paragraph, would fall to be imposed); or

    (b)   make a community service order within the meaning of section 238(1) of the 1995 Act (power to make such orders), so however that the total of all periods of unpaid work thus required in respect of the order is not to exceed forty hours (and accordingly any one such requirement will be for a period less than that which, but for this paragraph, would fall to be specified),

but the imposition of a sentence under paragraph (a) or making of an order under paragraph (b) does not of itself affect the drug treatment and testing order or probation order.

(5)   The Scottish Ministers may by order amend—

    (a)   paragraph (a) of subsection (4) by substituting, for the period of days; or

    (b)   paragraph (b) of that subsection, by substituting for the period of hours,

for the time being specified there as a period not to be exceeded, such other period of days, or as the case may be hours, as they think fit.

(6)   Where it is—

    (a)   alleged at—

(i)   a review hearing by a drugs court; or

(ii)   a diet of such a court to which an offender has been cited under section
       234G(1) of the 1995 Act (court actings in respect of breach of drug
       treatment and testing order),

that the offender has failed to comply with a requirement of a drug treatment and
testing order; or

(b)   alleged at—

(i)   a hearing by such a court, held by virtue of a requirement of a probation
       order, to review that order; or

(ii)   a diet of such a court to which a probationer has been cited under section
       232(1) or 233(1) of that Act (failure to comply with requirement of
       probation order and commission of further offence during probation
       period),

that the probationer has failed to comply with a requirement of a probation order,

that person shall forthwith be provided with written details of the alleged failure and
informed that there is an entitlement to be legally represented and that no answer need
be given as respects that allegation before an opportunity has been afforded the person
to take legal advice in that regard or the person has indicated that there is no wish to take
such advice.

(7)   If the offender or probationer denies the allegation, then only if, in accordance with
       section 232 or as the case may be 234G of the 1995 Act, that person's failure to comply
       is proved is the drugs court entitled to proceed as is mentioned in paragraph (a) or (b) of
       subsection (4).

(8)   If under section 234H of the 1995 Act (disposal on revocation of drug treatment and
       testing order) a drug treatment and testing order is revoked, the court (whether or not a
       drugs court) must, in imposing any sentence by virtue of subsection (1) of that section,
       take into account any—

(a)   sentence which has been imposed under paragraph (a) of subsection (4); or

(b)   order which has been made under paragraph (b) of that subsection,

in relation to a failure to comply with a requirement of the drug treatment and testing
order.

(9)   A court (whether or not a drugs court) must, in imposing any sentence by virtue of
       section 232(2)(b) of the 1995 Act (power to sentence offender), take into account any—

(a)   sentence which has been imposed under paragraph (a) of subsection (4); or

(b)   order which has been made under paragraph (b) of that subsection,

in relation to a failure to comply with a requirement of the probation order in question.

(10)   In this section—

       "drug treatment and testing order" has the meaning given by section 234B(2) of
       the 1995 Act (power to make drug treatment and testing order);

       "probation order" has the meaning given by section 228(1) of that Act (power to
       make probation order); and

       "review hearing" is to be construed in accordance with section 234F(1)(b) of that
       Act (periodic review of drug treatment and testing order).

(11) In the 1995 Act—

   (a) in section 228(5)(b) (explanation to be given to offender of possible consequences of failure to comply with probation order), at the end there is added "or may be dealt with under the powers provided for in section 42(4) of the Criminal Justice (Scotland) Act 2003 (asp 7) (powers of drugs court)";

   (b) in section 232 (probation orders: failure to comply with requirement), at the end there is added—

     "(8) This section is subject to section 42(9) of the Criminal Justice (Scotland) Act 2003 (asp 7) (powers of drugs court).";

   (c) in section 234D(1)(b) (explanation to be given to offender of possible consequences of failure to comply with drug treatment and testing order), after the word "Act" there is inserted "or 42(4) of the Criminal Justice (Scotland) Act 2003 (asp 7) (powers of drugs court)"; and

   (d) in section 234H (disposal on revocation of drug treatment and testing order), at the end there is added—

     "(4) This section is subject to section 42(8) of the Criminal Justice (Scotland) Act 2003 (asp 7) (powers of drugs court).".

PART 6

NON-CUSTODIAL PUNISHMENTS

43 Restriction of liberty orders

(1) The 1995 Act is amended as follows.

(2) In section 245A(5)(a) (duty of clerk of court by which restriction of liberty order is made)—

   (a) the existing words "to any person who is to be responsible for monitoring the offender's compliance with the order" become sub-paragraph (i); and

   (b) after that sub-paragraph there is inserted the word "and" and the following sub-paragraph—

     "(ii) if the offender resides (or is to reside) in a place outwith the jurisdiction of the court making the order, to the clerk of a court within whose jurisdiction that place is;".

(3) In section 245E (variation of restriction of liberty order)—

   (a) in subsection (1)—

     (i) after the word "may" there are inserted the words "except in a case to which paragraph (b) below applies," and those words together with the existing words "apply to the court which made the order" become paragraph (a); and

     (ii) after that paragraph there is inserted the word "or" and the following paragraph—

"(b) where a copy of the order was, under section 245A(5)(a)(ii) of this Act or subsection (7)(a) below, sent to the clerk of a different court, to that different court (or, if there has been more than one such sending, the different court to which such a copy has most recently been so sent),"; and

(b) at the end there is added—

"(5) Where a reason for an application by the offender under subsection (1) above is that he proposes to reside in a place outwith the jurisdiction of the court to which that application is made, and the court is satisfied that suitable arrangements can be made, in the district where that place is, for monitoring his compliance with the order it may—

(a) vary the order to permit or make practicable such arrangements; and

(b) where the change in residence necessitates or makes desirable a change in who is designated for the purpose of such monitoring, vary the order accordingly.

(6) Before varying a restriction of liberty order for the reason mentioned in subsection (5) above, the court shall—

(a) if the order will require the offender to remain in a specified place or in specified places, obtain and consider information about that place, or those places, including information as to the attitude of persons likely to be affected by any enforced presence there of the offender; and

(b) satisfy itself that his compliance with that requirement can be monitored by the means of monitoring specified, or which it intends to specify, in the order.

(7) Where a restriction of liberty order is varied as is mentioned in subsection (5) above, the clerk of the court shall send a copy of the order as so varied to—

(a) the clerk of a court within whose jurisdiction the place of proposed residence is;

(b) the person who, immediately before the order was varied, was responsible for monitoring the person's compliance with it; and

(c) the person who, in consequence of the variation, is to have that responsibility.

(8) If, in relation to an application made for such reason as is mentioned in subsection (5) above, the court is not satisfied as is mentioned in that subsection, it may—

(a) refuse the application; or

(b) revoke the order.".

(4) In section 245F (breach of restriction of liberty order)—

(a) in subsection (1)—

(i) after the words "force it appears", there is inserted "except in a case to which paragraph (b) below applies," and those words together with the existing words "to the court which made the order" become paragraph (a);

(ii) after that paragraph there is inserted the word "or" and the following paragraph—

"(b) where a copy of the order was, under section 245A(5)(a)(ii) or 245E(7)(a) of this Act, sent to the clerk of a different court, to that different court (or, if there has been more than one such sending, the different court to which such a copy has most recently been so sent),";

(iii) after the words "order the court" there is inserted "in question";

(iv) for the words "the court", where they occur for the third time, there is substituted "it"; and

(v) for the words "the court", where they occur for the fourth time, there is substituted "that court";

(b) in subsection (2), for the words—

(i) "the court", where they occur for the first time, there is substituted "that court"; and

(ii) "the court", where they occur for the second time, there is substituted "it"; and

(c) in subsection (4), for the words "the court" there is substituted "a court".

44   Interim anti-social behaviour orders

(1) In section 19 of the Crime and Disorder Act 1998 (c.37) (anti-social behaviour orders), after subsection (2) there is inserted—

"(2A) On an application made under subsection (1) above, being an application of which the person in respect of whom it is made has received intimation, the sheriff may, pending its determination, make such interim order as the sheriff considers appropriate provided that he is satisfied—

(a) that were the actings or conduct complained of in the application established, the condition mentioned in paragraph (a) of that subsection would be fulfilled; and

(b) that such an interim order is necessary for the purpose mentioned in paragraph (b) of that subsection.".

(2) In section 21 of that Act (procedural provisions with respect to orders)—

(a) in subsection (6), after the word "section" there is inserted "19(2A) or"; and

(b) after subsection (9) there is inserted—

"(9A) An interlocutor granting or refusing, under section 19(2A) above, an interim order is an appealable interlocutor.

(9B) Where an appeal is taken, by virtue of subsection (9A) above, against an interlocutor granting an interim order that order shall, without prejudice to any power of the court to vary or recall it, continue to have effect pending the disposal of the appeal.".

(3) In section 22 of that Act (offences in connection with breach of orders)—

(a) in subsection (1), after the words "anti-social behaviour order" there is inserted ", or an interim order under section 19(2A) above,";

(b) in subsection (2)(a), the words "anti-social behaviour" are repealed;

(c) in each of subsections (3)(a) and (4), for the words "an anti-social behaviour order" there is substituted "the order so referred to"; and

(d) in subsection (6), after the words "in relation to" where they occur for the second time, there is inserted "an order under section 19(2A) above and to".

45 Application by registered social landlord for anti-social behaviour order

(1) The Crime and Disorder Act 1998 (c.37) is amended as follows.

(2) In section 19 (anti-social behaviour orders)—

  (a) in subsection (1)—

    (i) for the word "local" there is substituted "relevant";

    (ii) in paragraph (a), the words "in the authority's area" are repealed; and

    (iii) in paragraph (b), for the words "persons in the authority's area" there is substituted "relevant persons";

  (b) in subsection (3), for the words "persons in the area of the local authority" there is substituted "relevant persons";

  (c) in subsection (6), for the word "local" there is substituted "relevant"; and

  (d) for subsection (8) there is substituted—

"(8) In this section and section 21 below—

"relevant authority" means—

  (a) a local authority (that is to say, a council constituted under section 2 of the Local Government etc. (Scotland) Act 1994 (c.39)); or

  (b) a body registered in the register maintained under section 57 of the Housing (Scotland) Act 2001 (asp 10) (the register of social landlords);

"relevant person" means, in relation to an application by—

  (a) a local authority, a person in the area of that authority;

  (b) a registered social landlord—

    (i) a person residing in, or otherwise on or likely to be on, premises provided or managed by that landlord; or

    (ii) a person in, or likely to be in, the vicinity of such premises;

and any reference to the area of a local authority is a reference to the local government area (within the meaning of the said Act of 1994) for which that authority is constituted.".

(3) In section 21 (procedural provisions with respect to orders)—

  (a) in subsection (1), for the words " the local" there is substituted "a relevant";

  (b) in subsection (2)—

    (i) for the word "the" where it first occurs there is substituted "a"; and

    (ii) for the words "the order is sought is for the time being" there is substituted "the application is to be made resides or appears to reside";

  (c) after subsection (2) there is inserted—

"(2A) Before making an application under section 19(1) above or subsection (7)(b)(i) below, a registered social landlord shall provide notification of its intention to do so to the local authority within whose area the person in respect of whom the application is to be made resides or appears to reside.";

(d) in subsection (3)—

   (i) the existing words from "the area of which" to the end become paragraph (a); and

   (ii) after that paragraph there is added the word "or" and the following paragraph—

      "(b) as the case may be, the place where the person in relation to whom the application is to be made by the registered social landlord resides or appears to reside"; and

(e) in subsection (7)(b)(i), after the word "constable" there is inserted "or registered social landlord".

46   Requirement for remote monitoring in probation order

(1) The 1995 Act is amended as follows.

(2) After section 230 there is inserted—

"230A   Requirement for remote monitoring in probation order

   (1) Without prejudice to section 245D of this Act, a probation order may include a requirement that during such period as may be specified in the requirement, being a period not exceeding twelve months, the probationer comply with such restrictions as to his movements as the court thinks fit; and paragraphs (a) and (b) of subsection (2) of section 245A of this Act (with the qualification of paragraph (a) which that subsection contains) shall apply in relation to any such requirement as they apply in relation to a restriction of liberty order.

   (2) The clerk of the court shall cause a copy of a probation order which includes such a requirement to be sent to the person who is to be responsible for monitoring the probationer's compliance with the requirement.

   (3) If, within the period last specified by virtue of subsection (1) above or section 231(1) of this Act, it appears to the person so responsible that the probationer has failed to comply with the requirement the person shall so inform the supervising officer appointed by virtue of section 228(3) of this Act, who shall report the matter to the court.

   (4) Section 245H shall apply in relation to proceedings under section 232 of this Act as respects a probation order which includes such a requirement as it applies in relation to proceedings under section 245F of this Act.

   (5) Sections 245A(6) and (8) to (11), 245B and 245C of this Act shall apply in relation to the imposition of, or as the case may be compliance with, requirements included by virtue of subsection (1) above in a probation order as those sections apply in relation to the making of, or as the case may be compliance with, a restriction of liberty order.

   (6) In relation to a probation order which includes such a requirement—

      (a) the persons who may make an application under paragraph 3(1) of Schedule 6 to this Act shall include the person responsible for monitoring the probationer's compliance with the requirement, but only in so far as the application relates to the requirement; and

      (b) a copy of any application under that paragraph by—

          (i) the probationer or the supervising officer shall be sent by the applicant to the person so responsible; or

          (ii) the person so responsible shall be sent by the applicant to the probationer and the supervising officer.

(7) Where under section 232(2)(c) of, or Schedule 6 to, this Act the court varies such a requirement, the clerk of court shall cause a copy of the amended probation order to be sent—

      (a) to the person so responsible; and

      (b) where the variation comprises a change in who is designated for the purposes of such monitoring, to the person who, immediately before the order was varied, was so responsible.".

(3) In section 232 (probation orders: failure to comply with requirement)—

      (a) in subsection (2)(c), at the end there is added "and any extension to the period of a requirement imposed by virtue of section 230A of this Act shall not increase that period above the maximum mentioned in subsection (1) of that section"; and

      (b) after subsection (2) there is inserted—

"(2A) Subsections (6) and (11) of section 245A of this Act apply to the variation, under paragraph (c) of subsection (2) above, of a requirement such as is mentioned in that paragraph as they apply to the making of a restriction of liberty order.".

(4) In Schedule 6 (discharge of and amendment to probation orders), in paragraph 3—

      (a) in sub-paragraph (1), for the words "230" there is substituted "230A"; and

      (b) at the end there is added—

"(3) This paragraph is subject to section 230A(6)(a) of this Act.".

47   Requirement for remote monitoring in drug treatment and testing order

(1) The 1995 Act is amended as follows.

(2) After section 234C there is inserted—

"234CA Requirement for remote monitoring in drug treatment and testing order

(1) A drug treatment and testing order may include a requirement that during such period as may be specified in the requirement, being a period not exceeding twelve months, the offender comply with such restrictions as to his movements as the court thinks fit; and paragraphs (a) and (b) of subsection (2) of section 245A of this Act (with the qualification of paragraph (a) which that subsection contains) shall apply in relation to any such requirement as they apply in relation to a restriction of liberty order.

(2) The clerk of the court shall cause a copy of a drug treatment and testing order which includes such a requirement to be sent to the person who is to be responsible for monitoring the offender's compliance with the requirement.

(3) If, within the period last specified by virtue of subsection (1) above or (6)(d) below, it appears to the person so responsible that the offender has failed to comply with the requirement the person shall so inform the supervising officer appointed by virtue of section 234C(6) of this Act, who shall report the matter to the court.

(4) Section 245H shall apply in relation to proceedings under section 234G of this Act as respects a drug treatment and testing order which includes such a requirement as it applies in relation to proceedings under section 245F of this Act.

(5) Sections 245A(6) and (8) to (11), 245B and 245C of this Act shall apply in relation to the imposition of, or as the case may be compliance with, requirements included by virtue of subsection (1) above in a drug treatment and testing order as those sections apply in relation to the making of, or as the case may be compliance with, a restriction of liberty order.

(6) In relation to a drug testing order which includes such a requirement, section 234E of this Act shall apply with the following modifications—

    (a) the persons who may make an application under subsection (1) of that section shall include the person responsible for monitoring the offender's compliance with the requirement, but only in so far as the application relates to the requirement;

    (b) the reference in subsection (2) of that section to the supervising officer shall be construed as a reference to either that officer or the person so responsible;

    (c) where an application is made under subsection (1) of that section and relates to the requirement, the persons to be heard under subsection (3) of that section shall include the person so responsible;

    (d) the ways of varying the order which are mentioned in subsection (3)(a) of that section shall include increasing or decreasing the period specified by virtue of subsection (1) above (or last specified by virtue of this paragraph) but not so as to increase that period above the maximum mentioned in subsection (1) above; and

    (e) the reference in subsection (5) of that section—

        (i) to the supervising officer shall be construed as a reference to either that officer or the person so responsible; and

        (ii) to sections 234B(5) and 234D(1) shall be construed as including a reference to section 245A(6) and (11).

(7) Where under section 234E or 234G(2)(b) of this Act the court varies such a requirement, the clerk of court shall cause a copy of the amended drug treatment and testing order to be sent—

    (a) to the person responsible for monitoring the offender's compliance with the requirement; and

(b) where the variation comprises a change in who is designated for the purposes of such monitoring, to the person who, immediately before the order was varied, was so responsible.".

(3) In section 234E (amendment of drug treatment and testing order), at the end there is added—

"(7) This section is subject to section 234CA(6) of this Act.".

(4) In section 234G (breach of drug treatment and testing order)—

(a) in subsection (2)(b), at the end there is added "so however that any extension of the period of a requirement imposed by virtue of section 234CA of this Act shall not increase that period above the maximum mentioned in subsection (1) of that section"; and

(b) after subsection (2) there is inserted—

"(2A) Subsections (6) and (11) of section 245A of this Act apply to the variation, under paragraph (b) of subsection (2) above, of a requirement imposed as is mentioned in that paragraph as they apply to the making of a restriction of liberty order.".

48   Breach of certain orders: adjourning hearing and remanding in custody etc.

After section 245I of the 1995 Act there is inserted—

"**245J   Breach of certain orders: adjourning hearing and remanding in custody etc.**

(1) Where a probationer or offender appears before the court in respect of his apparent failure to comply with a requirement of, as the case may be, a probation order, drug treatment and testing order, supervised attendance order, community service order or restriction of liberty order the court may, for the purpose of enabling inquiries to be made or of determining the most suitable method of dealing with him, adjourn the hearing.

(2) Where, under subsection (1) above, the court adjourns a hearing it shall remand the probationer or offender in custody or on bail or ordain him to appear at the adjourned hearing.

(3) A court shall not so adjourn a hearing for any single period exceeding four weeks or, on cause shown, eight weeks.

(4) A probationer or offender remanded under this section may appeal against the refusal of bail, or against the conditions imposed, within 24 hours of his remand.

(5) Any such appeal shall be by note of appeal presented to the High Court, who, either in court or in chambers, may after hearing the prosecutor and the appellant—

(a) review the order appealed against and either grant bail on such conditions as it thinks fit or ordain the appellant to appear at the adjourned hearing; or

(b) confirm the order.".

49   Power of arrest where breach of non-harassment order

(1)   In section 234A (non-harassment orders) of the 1995 Act—

    (a) in subsection (4), the words "found to be" are repealed;

    (b) after that subsection there is inserted—

"(4A) A constable may arrest without warrant any person he reasonably believes is committing or has committed an offence under subsection (4) above.

(4B) Subsection (4A) above is without prejudice to any power of arrest conferred by law apart from that subsection.".

(2)   In section 9 (breach of non-harassment order) of the Protection from Harassment Act 1997 (c.40)—

    (a) in subsection (1), the words "found to be" are repealed;

    (b) after subsection (2) there is inserted—

"(3)   A constable may arrest without warrant any person he reasonably believes is committing or has committed an offence under subsection (1).

(4)   Subsection (3) is without prejudice to any power of arrest conferred by law apart from that subsection.".

50   Amendments in relation to certain non-custodial sentences

(1)   In section 235 (supervised attendance orders) of the 1995 Act—

    (a) in subsection (3)(a); and

    (b) in subsection (4)(b),

for the word "18" there is in each case substituted "16".

(2)   In section 236 (supervised attendance orders in place of fines) of that Act—

    (a) in subsection (1), for the words "16 or 17" there is substituted "or over 16";

    (b) in subsection (6), after "shall" there is inserted—

"(a) if it considers that the person is likely to pay the fine within a reasonable period of more than 28 days, impose the fine;

(b) in any other case".

(3)   In section 245A (restriction of liberty orders) of that Act, in subsection (1)—

    (a) after "offence" in the first place where it appears there is inserted "punishable by imprisonment";

    (b) the words from ", if" to "disposal," are repealed;

    (c) after "may" there is inserted ", instead of imposing on him a sentence of, or including, imprisonment or any other form of detention,".

(4)   In Schedule 7 (which makes further provision in respect of supervised attendance orders) to that Act—

    (a) in paragraph 4(2)(a)—

        (i)   for the words "three months" there is substituted "30 days";

        (ii)   for the words "60 days" there is substituted "20 days";

(b) in paragraph 5(1)(d)—

  (i)   for the words "three months" there is substituted "30 days";

  (ii) for the words "60 days" there is substituted "20 days".

PART 7

CHILDREN

51   Physical punishment of children

(1)   Where a person claims that something done to a child was a physical punishment carried out in exercise of a parental right or of a right derived from having charge or care of the child, then in determining any question as to whether what was done was, by virtue of being in such exercise, a justifiable assault a court must have regard to the following factors—

  (a)   the nature of what was done, the reason for it and the circumstances in which it took place;

  (b)   its duration and frequency;

  (c)   any effect (whether physical or mental) which it has been shown to have had on the child;

  (d)   the child's age; and

  (e)   the child's personal characteristics (including, without prejudice to the generality of this paragraph, sex and state of health) at the time the thing was done.

(2)   The court may also have regard to such other factors as it considers appropriate in the circumstances of the case.

(3)   If what was done included or consisted of—

  (a)   a blow to the head;

  (b)   shaking; or

  (c)   the use of an implement,

the court must determine that it was not something which, by virtue of being in exercise of a parental right or of a right derived as is mentioned in subsection (1), was a justifiable assault; but this subsection is without prejudice to the power of the court so to determine on whatever other grounds it thinks fit.

(4)   In subsection (1), "child" means a person who had not, at the time the thing was done, attained the age of sixteen years.

(5)   In section 12 of the Children and Young Persons (Scotland) Act 1937 (c.37) (cruelty to persons under sixteen)—

  (a)   in subsection (1), the words "assaults," and "assaulted," are repealed; and

  (b)   subsection (7) is repealed.

52   Prohibition of publication of proceedings at children's hearing etc.

In the Children (Scotland) Act 1995 (c. 36)—

    (a) in section 44 (prohibition of publication of proceedings at children's hearing), in subsection (1)—

        (i) after the word "publish" there is inserted "any matter in respect of a case about which the Principal Reporter has from any source received information or"; and

        (ii) in paragraph (a), for the words "any child concerned in the" there is substituted "the child concerned in, or any other child connected (in any way) with, the case,"; and

    (b) in section 93 (interpretation of Part II), in subsection (2)—

        (i) in paragraph (a), after the word "Part" there is inserted "and section 44"; and

        (ii) in paragraph (b), for the words "Chapters 2 and" there is substituted "Chapter 2 (except section 44) and Chapter".

53   Provision by Principal Reporter of information to victims

(1) Where the Principal Reporter has received information about a case in which it appears that an offence has been committed by a child, the Principal Reporter may provide any information about the case as is mentioned in subsection (2) to any person mentioned in subsection (3) if (and only if)—

    (a) the information is requested by the person; and

    (b) the Principal Reporter is satisfied that—

        (i) the provision of the information would not be detrimental to the best interests of the child concerned in, or any other child connected (in any way) with, the case; and

        (ii) it is appropriate in the circumstances of the case to provide the information.

(2) The information is information as to—

    (a) what action the Principal Reporter has taken in the case; and

    (b) any disposal of the case,

in so far as the information relates to the offence.

(3) The persons are—

    (a) any person against whom the offence appears to have been committed or, where that person is a child, any relevant person; and

    (b) any other person or class of persons, subject to such conditions, as may be prescribed.

(4) In this section—

    "child" means a person who has not attained the age of eighteen years;

    "the Principal Reporter" has the same meaning as it has in Part II of the Children (Scotland) Act 1995 (c.36);

    "relevant person" in relation to a child means—

        (a) any parent enjoying parental responsibilities or parental rights under Part I of that Act;

   (b)   any person in whom parental responsibilities or rights are vested by, under or by virtue of that Act; and

   (c)   any person who appears to be a person who ordinarily (and other than by reason only of that person's employment) has charge of, or control over, the child.

PART 8

EVIDENTIAL, JURISDICTIONAL AND PROCEDURAL MATTERS

Evidential matters

54   Certificates relating to physical data: sufficiency of evidence

In section 284(2) of the 1995 Act (no entitlement to challenge sufficiency of evidence in certificate relating to certain physical data), for the words "such other party shall not be entitled to challenge the sufficiency of the evidence contained within the certificate" there is substituted ", if that other party serves on the first party, not more than seven days after the date of service of the copy on him, a notice that he does not accept the evidence contained in the certificate, subsection (1) above shall not apply in relation to that evidence.".

55   Taking samples by swabbing

   (1)   The 1995 Act is amended as follows.

   (2)   In section 18 (prints, samples etc. in criminal investigations)—

      (a) in subsection (6), paragraph (d) is repealed; and

      (b) after that subsection there is inserted—

      "(6A) A constable, or at a constable's direction a police custody and security officer, may take from the inside of the person's mouth, by means of swabbing, a sample of saliva or other material.".

   (3)   In each of sections 19(2) (prints, samples etc. in criminal investigations: supplementary provisions) and 19A(2) (samples etc. from persons convicted of sexual and violent offences)—

      (a) the word "and" which immediately follows paragraph (a) is repealed;

      (b) in paragraph (b), for the word "(d)" there is substituted "(c)"; and

      (c) after that paragraph there is added the word "and" and the following paragraph—

         "(c) take, or direct a police custody and security officer to take, from the person any sample mentioned in subsection (6A) of that section by the means specified in that subsection.".

   (4)   In section 19B (power of constable in obtaining relevant physical data etc.), the existing provisions become subsection (1); and after that subsection there is added—

      "(2) A constable may, with the authority of an officer of a rank no lower than inspector, use reasonable force in (himself) exercising any power conferred by section 18(6A), 19(2)(c) or 19A(2)(c) of this Act.".

56   Retaining sample or relevant physical data where given voluntarily

(1)   This section applies only to a person other than is mentioned in subsection (1) of section 18 of the 1995 Act (application of that section) and does not apply where a sample is, or relevant physical data are, taken from a person—

    (a)   by virtue of any power of search;

    (b)   by virtue of any power to take possession of evidence where there is imminent danger of its being lost or destroyed; or

    (c)   under the authority of a warrant.

(2)   In the circumstances mentioned in subsection (3), a sample or relevant physical data taken from and with the consent of the person (or provided by and with the consent of the person) in connection with the investigation of an offence may be held and used in connection with the investigation and prosecution of that or any other offence as may any information derived from that sample or those data.

(3)   The circumstances are that the person consents in writing to the sample, data or information being so held and used; but in giving such consent the person may elect to confine it to consent to holding and using in connection with the investigation and prosecution of the offence in connection with which the sample was, or data were, taken or provided.

(4)   The person may at any time withdraw such written consent by—

    (a)   giving notice in writing of such withdrawal to the chief constable of the police force on whose behalf the sample was, or data were, taken or provided; or

    (b)   attending at any police station within the area of that force and giving such notice to—

        (i)   any constable of the force; or

        (ii)   any person authorised to receive it by the officer in charge of the station,

and the chief constable, constable or as the case may be person so authorised shall, on receipt of that notice, provide the person withdrawing consent with a written acknowledgment of receipt.

(5)   The withdrawal takes effect when notice given under subsection (4) is received by the person to whom it falls to provide an acknowledgment under that subsection; and subject to subsection (6)—

    (a)   the sample, with all information derived from it, is;

    (b)   the data, with all information derived from them, are,

to be destroyed as soon as possible after such receipt.

(6)   Subsections (4) and (5) are without prejudice to—

    (a)   the use of the sample, data or information derived from it or them in evidence—

        (i)   unless an election was made under subsection (3), in any prosecution; and

        (ii)   if such an election was so made, in the prosecution of the offence in connection with which the sample was, or data were, taken or provided,

        where and in so far as that evidence relates to, or to circumstances connected with or arising out of, a check such as is mentioned in subsection (7);

    (b)   the admissibility of any evidence as to—

        (i)   the taking or provision of the sample or data; or

        (ii)   the giving or withdrawal of consent.

(7)   The check is one which—

      (a)   was against any other sample or relevant physical data, or against any information derived from any other sample or relevant physical data; and

      (b)   took place before the withdrawal took effect.

(8)   In this section—

        "sample" means a sample such as is mentioned in section 18(6) or (6A) of the 1995 Act, being one taken as so mentioned; and

        "relevant physical data" has the same meaning as it has for the purposes of section 18 of that Act.

57   Convictions in other member States of the European Union

(1)   The 1995 Act is amended as follows.

(2)   In section 101(8) (manner of proving previous conviction in solemn proceedings)—

      (a)   after the words "section 285" there is inserted ", or as the case may be 286A,"; and

      (b)   for the words "said section" there is substituted "section in question".

(3)   In section 286 (proof of previous conviction in support of substantive charge), at the end there is added—

        "(3)   The reference in subsection (1)(a) above to "the clerk of court having custody of the record containing the conviction" includes, in relation to a previous conviction by a court in another member State of the European Union, a reference to any officer of that court or of that State having such custody.".

(4)   After section 286 there is inserted—

"286A   Proof of previous conviction by court in other member State

     (1)   A previous conviction by a court in another member State of the European Union may be proved against any person in any criminal proceedings by the production of evidence of the conviction and by showing that his fingerprints and those of the person convicted are the fingerprints of the same person.

     (2)   A certificate—

        (a)   bearing—

           (i)   to have been sealed with the official seal of a Minister of the State in question; and

           (ii)   to contain particulars relating to a conviction extracted from the criminal records of that State; and

        (b)   including copies of fingerprints and certifying that those copies—

           (i)   are of fingerprints appearing from those records to have been taken from the person convicted on the occasion of the conviction, or on the occasion of his last conviction; and

> > (ii)   would be admissible in evidence in criminal proceedings in that State as a record of the skin of that person's fingers,

> shall be sufficient evidence of the conviction or, as the case may be, of the person's last conviction and of all preceding convictions and that the copies of the fingerprints included in the certificate are copies of the fingerprints of the person convicted.

> (3)   A conviction bearing to have been—

> > (a)   extracted from the criminal records of the State in question; and

> > (b)   issued by an officer of that State whose duties include the issuing of such extracts,

> shall be received in evidence without being sworn to by witnesses.

> (4)   Subsection (9) of section 285 of this Act applies in relation to this section as it does in relation to that section.".

(5)   In section 307 (interpretation)—

> (a)   in subsection (1), in the definition of "extract conviction" and "extract of previous conviction", at the end there is added "and also include a conviction extracted and issued as mentioned in section 286A(3)(a) and (b) of this Act"; and

> (b)   in subsection (5), at the end there is added "except—

> > (a)   where the context otherwise requires; and

> > (b)   in sections 69(2) and 166, where such a reference includes a reference to a previous conviction, by a court in another member State of the European Union, of an act punishable under the law in force in that State (an act so punishable being taken to constitute an offence under that law however described in that law)".

Jurisdictional matters

58   Transfer of sheriff court proceedings

(1)   In section 83 of the 1995 Act (transfer of sheriff court solemn proceedings)—

> (a)   in subsection (1), for the words ", at any time before the commencement of his trial, apply to the sheriff to adjourn the trial and transfer it to a sitting of a sheriff court, appointed as mentioned in section 66(1) of this Act, in any other district in that sheriffdom" there is substituted "apply to the sheriff for an order for the transfer of the proceedings to a sheriff court in another district in that sheriffdom (that court being taken to be, by virtue of any such order, appointed as mentioned in section 66(1) of this Act) and for adjournment to a sitting of that court";

> (b)   after subsection (1) there is inserted—

> "(1A)   Where—

> > (a)   an accused person has been cited to attend a sitting of the sheriff court; or

> > (b)   paragraph (a) above does not apply but it is competent so to cite an accused person,

and the prosecutor is informed by the sheriff clerk that, because of exceptional circumstances which could not reasonably have been foreseen, it is not practicable for that court (in subsection (2A)(b)(i) below referred to as the "relevant court") or any other sheriff court in that sheriffdom to proceed with the case, the prosecutor—

   (i) may, where paragraph (b) above applies, so cite the accused; and

   (ii) shall, where paragraph (a) above applies or the accused is so cited by virtue of paragraph (i) above, as soon as practicable apply to the sheriff principal for an order for the transfer of the proceedings to a sheriff court in another sheriffdom (that court being taken to be, by virtue of any such order, appointed as mentioned in section 66(1) of this Act) and for adjournment to a sitting of that court.";

(c) in subsection (2), for the words "adjourn the trial and make an order for the transfer of the trial as mentioned in subsection (1) above" there is substituted "make such order as is mentioned in that subsection";

(d) after subsection (2) there is inserted—

"(2A) On an application under subsection (1A) above the sheriff principal may make the order sought—

   (a) provided that the sheriff principal of the other sheriffdom consents; but

   (b) in a case where the trial (or part of the trial) would be transferred, shall do so only—

     (i) if the sheriff of the relevant court, after giving the accused or his counsel an opportunity to be heard, consents to the transfer; or

     (ii) on the joint application of the parties.

(2B) On the application of the prosecutor, a sheriff principal who has made an order under subsection (2A) above may, if the sheriff principal of the other sheriffdom mentioned in that subsection consents—

   (a) revoke; or

   (ii) vary so as to restrict the effect of,

that order."; and

(e) in subsection (3), for the words from "the trial has been adjourned" to the end there is substituted "there has then been an order under subsection (2) or (2A) above, the warrant shall, subject to subsection (2B) above, have effect subject to the adjournment provided for in the order and as if the sitting is a sitting of the court to which the proceedings have been transferred".

(2)   After section 137 of that Act there is inserted—

"137A Transfer of sheriff court summary proceedings within sheriffdom

(1) Where an accused person has been cited to attend a diet of the sheriff court the prosecutor may apply to the sheriff for an order for the transfer of the proceedings to a sheriff court in any other district in that sheriffdom and for adjournment to a diet of that court.

(2) On an application under subsection (1) above the sheriff may make such order as is mentioned in that subsection.

137B   Transfer of sheriff court summary proceedings outwith sheriffdom

(1)   Where—

    (a)   an accused person has been cited to attend a diet of the sheriff court; or

    (b)   paragraph (a) does not apply but it is competent so to cite an accused person,

and the prosecutor is informed by the sheriff clerk that, because of exceptional circumstances which could not reasonably have been foreseen, it is not practicable for that court or any other sheriff court in that sheriffdom to proceed with the case, the prosecutor—

    (i)   may, where paragraph (b) above applies, so cite the accused; and

    (ii)   shall, where paragraph (a) above applies or the accused is so cited by virtue of paragraph (i) above, as soon as practicable apply to the sheriff principal for an order for the transfer of the proceedings to a sheriff court in another sheriffdom and for adjournment to a diet of that court.

(2)   On an application under subsection (1) above the sheriff principal may make the order sought, provided that the sheriff principal of the other sheriffdom consents.

(3)   On the application of the prosecutor, a sheriff principal who has made an order under subsection (2) above may, if the sheriff principal of the other sheriffdom mentioned in that subsection consents—

    (a)   revoke; or

    (b)   vary so as to restrict the effect of,

that order.".

59   Competence of justice's actings outwith jurisdiction

After section 9 of the 1995 Act there is inserted—

"9A   Competence of justice's actings outwith jurisdiction

It is competent for a justice, even if not present within his jurisdiction, to sign any warrant, judgment, interlocutor or other document relating to proceedings within that jurisdiction provided that when he does so he is present within Scotland.".

Procedural matters

60   Unified citation provisions

(1)   In the 1995 Act, in—

    (a)   section 232 (probation orders: failure to comply with requirement), for subsection (7) there is substituted;

    (b)   section 233 (probation orders: commission of further offence), after subsection (1) there is inserted;

    (c)   section 234E (amendment of drug treatment and testing order), after subsection (2) there is inserted;

    (d)   section 234G (breach of drug treatment testing order), after subsection (1) there is inserted;

(e) section 239 (community service orders: requirements), after subsection (4) there is inserted;

(f) section 240 (community service orders: amendment and revocation etc.), at the end there is added;

(g) section 245E (variation of restriction of liberty order), after subsection (3) there is inserted; and

(h) section 245F (breach of restriction of liberty order), after subsection (1) there is inserted,

in each case as a subsection appropriately numbered, the following—

"( )   The unified citation provisions apply in relation to a citation under this section as they apply in relation to a citation under section 216(3)(a) of this Act.".

(2)   In section 307(1) of that Act (interpretation), at the appropriate place there is inserted—

""the unified citation provisions" means section 216(5) and (6)(a) and (b) of this Act;".

(3)   In Schedule 6 to that Act (discharge of and amendment to probation orders), in paragraph 5, at the end there is added—

"(3)   The unified citation provisions apply in relation to a citation under sub-paragraph (1) above as they apply in relation to a citation under section 216(3)(a) of this Act.".

(4)   In Schedule 7 to that Act (supervised attendance orders: further provisions), after paragraph 5, there is inserted—

"5A   The unified citation provisions apply in relation to a citation under paragraph 4(1) or 5(3) of this Schedule as they apply in relation to a citation under section 216(3)(a) of this Act.".

(5)   In section 15 of the 1993 Act (variation of supervised release order etc.), after subsection (5) there is inserted—

"(5A)   The unified citation provisions (as defined by section 307(1) of the Criminal Procedure (Scotland) Act 1995 (c.46)) apply in relation to a citation under subsection (5) above as they apply in relation to a citation under section 216(3)(a) of that Act.".

(6)   In section 18 of that Act (breach of supervised release order), after subsection (1) there is inserted—

"(1A)   The unified citation provisions (as defined by section 307(1) of the Criminal Procedure (Scotland) Act 1995 (c.46)) apply in relation to a citation under subsection (1)(b) above as they apply in relation to a citation under section 216(3)(a) of that Act.".

61   Citation other than by service of indictment or complaint

(1)   In section 66 of the 1995 Act (service and lodging of indictment etc.)—

(a)   for subsection (4) there is substituted—

"(4)   The accused may be cited either—

(a) by being served with a copy of the indictment and of the list of the names and addresses of the witnesses to be adduced by the prosecution; or

(b) by a constable affixing to the door of the accused's dwelling-house or place of business a notice in such form as may be prescribed by Act of Adjournal, or as nearly as may be in such form—

(i) specifying the date on which it was so affixed;

(ii) informing the accused that he may collect a copy of the indictment and of such list as is mentioned in paragraph (a) above from a police station specified in the notice; and

(iii) calling upon him to appear and answer to the indictment at such diet as shall be so specified.

(4A) Where a date is specified by virtue of sub-paragraph (i) of subsection (4)(b) above, that date shall be deemed the date on which the indictment is served; and the copy of the indictment referred to in sub-paragraph (ii) of that subsection shall, for the purposes of subsections (12) and (13) below be deemed the service copy.

(4B) Paragraphs (a) and (b) of subsection (6) below shall apply for the purpose of specifying a diet by virtue of subsection (4)(b)(iii) above as they apply for the purpose of specifying a diet in any notice under subsection (6).";

(b) in subsection (6)—

(i) for the words "Except where the indictment is served" there is substituted "If the accused is cited by being served with a copy of the indictment, then except where such service is"; and

(ii) in paragraph (b), the words "and notice" are repealed;

(c) in subsection (7), at the beginning there is inserted "Subject to subsection (4)(b) above,";

(d) in subsection (8), after the word "indictment" there is inserted ", to citation under subsection (4)(b) above";

(e) in subsection (11), after the word—

(i) "indictment" there is inserted ", or who executed a citation under subsection (4)(b) above,"; and

(ii) "service" there is inserted "or execution";

(f) in subsection (13), the words "required to be" are repealed; and

(g) in subsection (14)—

(i) for the word "of", in the second place where it occurs, there is substituted "or"; and

(ii) for the words "requiring to be" there is substituted "so".

(2) In section 140(2) of that Act (form of citation in summary proceedings), at the beginning there is inserted "Without prejudice to section 141(2A) of this Act,".

(3) In section 141 of that Act (manner of citation in such proceedings)—

(a) after subsection (2) there is inserted—

"(2A) Notwithstanding subsection (1) above and section 140(2) of this Act, citation of the accused may also be effected by an officer of law affixing to the door of the accused's dwelling-house or place of business a notice in such form as may be prescribed by Act of Adjournal, or as nearly as may be in such form—

    (a) specifying the date on which it was so affixed;

    (b) informing the accused that he may collect a copy of the complaint from a police station specified in the notice; and

    (c) calling upon him to appear and answer the complaint at such diet as shall be so specified.

(2B) Where the citation of the accused is effected by notice under subsection (2A) above, the induciae shall be reckoned from the date specified by virtue of paragraph (a) of that subsection.";

(b) in subsection (3), after the word "below" there is inserted "and without prejudice to the effect of any other manner of citation";

(c) in subsection (5), after the word "subsection", in the first place where it occurs, there is inserted "(2A) or"; and

(d) in subsection (7)—

    (i) the existing words from "a citation" to the end shall be paragraph (a); and

    (ii) after that paragraph there shall be added the word "; or" and the following paragraph—

      "(b) citation has been effected by notice under subsection (2A) above, if there is produced in court a written execution, in such form as may be prescribed by Act of Adjournal, or as nearly as may be in such form, signed by the officer of law who affixed the notice.".

62   Leave to appeal: extension of time limit for application under section 107(4) of 1995 Act

In section 107 of the 1995 Act (leave to appeal)—

(a) in subsection (3)—

    (i) after the words "subsection (4) below" there is inserted "(and if that period is extended under subsection (4A) below before the period being extended expires, until the expiry of the period as so extended)"; and

    (ii) for the words "that subsection" there is substituted "subsection (4)"; and

(b) after subsection (4) there is inserted—

"(4A) The High Court may, on cause shown, extend the period of 14 days mentioned in subsection (4) above, or that period as extended under this subsection, whether or not the period to be extended has expired (and if that period of 14 days has expired, whether or not it expired before section 62 of the Criminal Justice (Scotland) Act 2003 (asp 7) came into force).".

63   Adjournment at first diet in summary proceedings

(1) The 1995 Act is amended as follows.

(2) In section 144 (procedure at first diet), in subsection (9) after "145" there is inserted "or 145A".

(3) In section 145 (adjournment for inquiry at first calling), in subsection (1) for the words from the beginning to "Act," there is substituted "Where the accused is present".

(4) After section 145 there is inserted—

"145A   Adjournment at first calling to allow accused to appear etc.

(1) Without prejudice to section 150(1) to (7) of this Act, where the accused is not present at the first calling of the case in a summary prosecution, the court may (whether or not the prosecutor is able to provide evidence that the accused has been duly cited) adjourn the case under this section for such period as it considers appropriate; and subject to subsections (2) and (3) below, the court may from time to time so adjourn the case.

(2) An adjournment under this section shall be—

(a) for the purposes of allowing—

(i) the accused to appear in answer to the complaint; or

(ii) time for inquiry into the case; or

(b) for any other cause the court considers reasonable.

(3) No one period of adjournment under this section shall exceed 28 days.".

64   Review hearing of drug treatment and testing order

In section 234F of the 1995 Act (periodic review of drug treatment and testing order), after subsection (1) there is inserted—

"(1A)   A review hearing may be held whether or not the prosecutor elects to appear.".

65   Transcript of record

In section 94 of the 1995 Act (transcripts of record and documentary productions)—

(a) in subsection (2)—

(i) at the end of paragraph (a) there is added "or, subject to subsection (2B) below, the prosecutor"; and

(ii) in paragraph (b), after the word "person" there is inserted ", not being a person convicted at the trial,"; and

(b) after that subsection there is inserted—

"(2A)   If—

(a) on the written application of a person convicted at the trial and granted leave to appeal; and

(b) on cause shown,

a judge of the High Court so orders, the Clerk of Justiciary shall direct, on payment of such charges as are mentioned in paragraph (b) of subsection (2) above, that such a transcript be made and sent to that person.

(2B) Where, as respects any person convicted at the trial, the Crown Agent has received intimation under section 107(10) of this Act, the prosecutor shall not be entitled to make a request under subsection (2)(a) above; but if, on the written application of the prosecutor and on cause shown, a judge of the High Court so orders, the Clerk of Justiciary shall direct that such a transcript be made and sent to the prosecutor.

(2C) Any application under subsection (2A) above shall—

  (a) be made within 14 days after the date on which leave to appeal was granted or within such longer period after that date as a judge of the High Court may, on written application and on cause shown, allow; and

  (b) be intimated forthwith by the applicant to the prosecutor.

(2D) The prosecutor may, within 7 days after receiving intimation under subsection (2C)(b) above, make written representations to the court as respects the application under subsection (2A) above (the application being determined without a hearing).

(2E) Any application under subsection (2B) above shall—

  (a) be made within 14 days after the receipt of intimation mentioned in that subsection or within such longer period after that receipt as a judge of the High Court may, on written application and on cause shown, allow; and

  (b) be intimated forthwith by the prosecutor to the person granted leave to appeal.

(2F) The person granted leave to appeal may, within 7 days after receiving intimation under subsection (2E)(b) above, make written representations to the court as respects the application under subsection (2B) above (the application being determined without a hearing).".

66   Bail and related matters

(1) The 1995 Act is amended as follows.

(2) In section 103 (appeal sittings)—

  (a) after subsection (6) there is inserted—

  "(6A) Where a judge acting under subsection (5)(c) above grants an application by an appellant to exercise that power in his favour, the prosecutor shall be entitled to have the application determined by the High Court."; and

  (b) in subsection (7) for the words "and (6)" there is substituted ", (6) and (6A)".

(3) In section 105 (appeal against refusal of application), after subsection (4), there is inserted—

  "(4A) An application by a convicted person for a determination by the High Court of a decision of a judge acting under section 103(5)(c) of this Act to refuse to admit him to bail shall be intimated by him immediately and in writing to the Crown Agent.".

(4) After section 105 there is inserted—

"105A   **Appeal against granting of application**

(1)   Where the prosecutor desires a determination by the High Court as mentioned in subsection (6A) of section 103 of this Act, he shall apply to the judge immediately after the power in subsection (5)(c) of that section is exercised in favour of the appellant.

(2)   Where a judge acting under section 103(5)(c) of this Act has exercised that power in favour of the appellant but the prosecutor has made an application under subsection (1) above—

     (a)   the appellant shall not be liberated until the determination by the High Court; and

     (b)   that application by the prosecutor shall be heard not more than seven days after the making of the application,

and the Clerk of the Justiciary shall forward to the appellant the prescribed form for completion and return forthwith if he desires to be present at the hearing.

(3)   At a hearing and determination as mentioned in subsection (2) above, if the appellant—

     (a)   is not legally represented, he may be present;

     (b)   is legally represented, he shall not be entitled to be present without leave of the court.

(4)   If the appellant completes and returns the form mentioned in subsection (2) above indicating a desire to be present at the hearing, the form shall be deemed to be an application by the appellant for leave to be so present, and the Clerk of Justiciary, on receiving the form, shall take the necessary steps for placing the application before the court.

(5)   If the application to be present is refused by the court, the Clerk of Justiciary shall notify the appellant; and if the application is granted, he shall notify the appellant and the Governor of the prison where the applicant is in custody and the Scottish Ministers.

(6)   For the purposes of constituting a Court of Appeal, the judge who exercised the power in section 103(5)(c) of this Act in favour of the appellant may sit as a member of the court, and take part in determining the application of the prosecutor.".

(5)   In section 112 (admission of appellant to bail)—

     (a)   in subsection (1) for "subsection (2)" there is inserted "subsections (2), (2A) and (9)";

     (b)   for subsection (2) there is substituted—

     "(2)   The High Court shall not admit a convicted person to bail under subsection (1) above unless—

         (a)   the application for bail—

            (i)   states reasons why it should be granted; and

            (ii)   where he is the appellant and has not lodged a note of appeal in accordance with section 110(1)(a) of this Act, sets out the proposed grounds of appeal; and

    (b) the prosecutor has had an opportunity to be heard on the application.

(2A) Where—

    (a) the convicted person is the appellant and has not lodged a note of appeal in accordance with section 110(1)(a) of this Act; or

    (b) the Lord Advocate is the appellant,

the High Court shall not admit the convicted person to bail under subsection (1) above unless it considers there to be exceptional circumstances justifying admitting him to bail.";

(c) in subsection (6) for "subsection (7)" there is inserted "subsections (7) and (9)";

(d) in subsection (7)—

    (i) the words from "the application" to the end become paragraph (a); and

    (ii) after that paragraph there is inserted "and

        (b) where the appeal relates to conviction on indictment, the prosecutor has had an opportunity to be heard on the application."; and

(e) after subsection (8) there is added—

"(9) An application for the purposes of subsection (1) or (6) above by a person convicted on indictment shall be—

    (a) intimated by him immediately and in writing to the Crown Agent; and

    (b) heard not less than seven days after the date of that intimation.".

67 Adjournment of case before sentence

In section 201 (power of court to adjourn case before sentence) of the 1995 Act, in subsection (3), for the words from "exceeding" to the end there is substituted "exceeding four weeks or, on cause shown, eight weeks.".

PART 9

BRIBERY AND CORRUPTION

68 Bribery and corruption: foreign officers etc.

(1) In determining whether actings which consist of offering or accepting a bribe constitute a crime at common law, it is immaterial that the functions of the person who receives or is offered the bribe—

    (a) have no connection with;

    (b) are carried out in a country or territory outwith,

the United Kingdom.

(2) The enactments mentioned in subsections (2) to (4) of section 108 of the Anti-terrorism, Crime and Security Act 2001 (c.24) (bribery and corruption: foreign officers etc.) are respectively amended as provided for in those subsections.

69   Bribery and corruption committed outwith UK

(1)   This section applies in a case where a national of the United Kingdom, a Scottish partnership or a body incorporated under the law of any part of the United Kingdom, does anything in a country or territory outwith the United Kingdom which, if done in Scotland, would constitute—

   (a)   as a crime at common law, bribery or accepting a bribe; or

   (b)   an offence mentioned in subsection (3).

(2)   In such a case—

   (a)   the thing done constitutes the crime or offence in question;

   (b)   where the thing done is done by a Scottish partnership and is proved to have been done with the consent or connivance of, or to be attributable to any neglect on the part of, a partner, he as well as the partnership is guilty of the crime or offence so constituted and is liable to be proceeded against and punished accordingly; and

   (c)   subsection (3) of section 11 of the 1995 Act (jurisdiction in relation to certain offences committed outwith Scotland) is to apply in respect of that national, partnership, partner or body as if the crime or offence were an offence to which that section applies.

(3)   The offences are—

   (a)   those under section 1 of the Public Bodies Corrupt Practices Act 1889 (c.69) (corruption in office); and

   (b)   the first two offences under section 1 of the Prevention of Corruption Act 1906 (c.34) (bribes obtained by or given to agents).

(4)   In subsection (1), "national of the United Kingdom" means an individual who is—

   (a)   a British citizen, a British Dependent Territories citizen, a British National (Overseas) or a British Overseas citizen;

   (b)   a person who under the British Nationality Act 1981 (c.61) is a British subject; or

   (c)   a British protected person within the meaning of that Act.

PART 10

CRIMINAL RECORDS

70   Registration for criminal records purposes

(1)   The Police Act 1997 (c.50) is amended as follows.

(2)   After section 120 there is inserted—

"120A   Refusal and cancellation of registration: Scotland

   (1)   The Scottish Ministers may refuse to include a person in, or may remove a person from, a register maintained under section 120 for the purposes of this Part if it appears to them that the registration of that person is likely to make it possible for information to become available to an individual who, in their opinion, is not a suitable person to have access to that information.

(2)   The Scottish Ministers may also remove a person from any such register if it appears to them that the registration of that person has resulted in information becoming known to such an individual.

(3)   In determining, for the purposes of this section, whether an individual is a suitable person to have access to information, the Scottish Ministers may have regard, in particular, to—

    (a)   any information relating to the individual which concerns a relevant matter ("relevant matter" having the same meaning as in section 113);

    (b)   whether that person is included in any list mentioned in section 113(3C);

    (c)   any information provided to them under subsection (4);

    (d)   any information provided to them by the chief officer of a police force in England and Wales or Northern Ireland in response to a request by them for such information as is available to that officer, relates to any such matter as is mentioned in paragraph (b) of subsection (4) and concerns such matter as is mentioned in paragraph (c) of that subsection;

    (e)   anything which has been done—

        (i)   under subsection (1) or (2) or section 122(3); or

        (ii)   in England and Wales or Northern Ireland under the provisions of this Act which apply in England and Wales or Northern Ireland and correspond to subsection (1) or (2),

    and any information on the basis of which that thing was done.

(4)   A chief constable of a police force in Scotland shall comply, as soon as practicable after receiving it, with any request by the Scottish Ministers to provide them with information which—

    (a)   is available to him;

    (b)   relates to—

        (i)   an applicant for registration under section 120;

        (ii)   a person so registered;

        (iii) an individual who is likely to have access to information in consequence of the countersigning of applications by a particular applicant for such registration or by a particular person so registered; and

    (c)   concerns a matter which they have notified the chief constable is a matter which in their opinion is relevant to the determination of the suitability of individuals for having access to information which may be provided by virtue of this Part.

(5)   The Scottish Ministers shall pay to a police authority the prescribed fee for information which the authority provide—

    (a)   as mentioned in subsection (3)(d); or

    (b)   in accordance with subsection (4).".

(3)   In section 115 (enhanced criminal record certificates)—

    (a)   in subsection (2)—

    (i)   the word "or", which immediately follows paragraph (a), is omitted; and

    (ii) at the end of paragraph (b) there is added "or

        (c) in relation to an individual to whom any of subsections (6C) to (6G) applies.";

  (b) in subsection (5), after paragraph (h) there is added—

        "(i) an assessment, investigation or review by an adoption agency or local authority as to the suitability of a person, whether or not the person in respect of whom the certificate is sought, to adopt a child (this paragraph being construed in accordance with sections 1(3A) and (4) and 65(1) of the Adoption (Scotland) Act 1978 (c.28) and as if it were one of the provisions of that Act listed in the definition of "adoption agency" in the said section 65(1))";

  (c) after subsection (6B) there is inserted—

"(6C) This subsection applies to an individual included or seeking inclusion in any list prepared for the purposes of Part II of the National Health Service (Scotland) Act 1978 (c.29) of—

    (a) medical practitioners undertaking to provide general medical services;

    (b) dental practitioners undertaking to provide general dental services;

    (c) medical practitioners and ophthalmic opticians undertaking to provide general ophthalmic services; or

    (d) persons undertaking to provide pharmaceutical services.

  (6D) This subsection applies to an individual who is—

    (a) a director of a body corporate included or seeking inclusion in a list referred to in subsection (6C)(c) or (d); or

    (b) a partner of a partnership included or seeking inclusion in a list so referred to.

  (6E) This subsection applies to an individual included or seeking inclusion in any list prepared by virtue of—

    (a) section 17EA of the National Health Service (Scotland) Act 1978 (services lists); or

    (b) section 24B of that Act (supplementary lists),

and to an individual included or seeking inclusion in such other list prepared for the purposes of Part I or Part II of that Act as may be prescribed.

  (6F) This subsection applies to an individual appointed or seeking appointment—

    (a) as one of Her Majesty's inspectors (as defined by section 135(1) of the Education (Scotland) Act 1980 (c.44)); or

    (b) by the Scottish Ministers, for the purposes of section 66 of that Act of 1980 (inspection of educational establishments) or of section 9 of the Standards in Scotland's Schools etc. Act 2000 (asp 6) (inspection of education authority).

  (6G) This subsection applies to an individual appointed or seeking appointment—

   (a) under section 39(2) of the Children (Scotland) Act 1995 (c.36) (formation of children's panel etc.) as a member of—

      (i) a children's panel;

      (ii) the Children's Panel Advisory Committee other than as chairman of that committee; or

      (iii) a joint advisory committee other than as chairman of such a committee;

   (b) by virtue of paragraph 7(b) of Schedule 1 to that Act of 1995 (appointment to sub-committee of Children's Panel Advisory Committee of person who is not a member of that Committee);

   (c) as the Principal Reporter or under section 128(4) of the Local Government etc. (Scotland) Act 1994 (c.39) as an officer to assist that officer;

   (d) as a prosecutor, as defined by section 307(1) of the Criminal Procedure (Scotland) Act 1995 (c.46), or as an officer to assist a prosecutor or to assist in the work of the Crown Office; or

   (e) in a panel established by virtue of section 101(1) of the Children (Scotland) Act 1995 (panels for curators *ad litem*, reporting officers and safeguarders).

(6H) Subsection (2) applies in relation to an exempted question asked in relation to an individual appointed or seeking appointment as mentioned in subsection (6G)(a) as it applies in relation to such a question asked in relation to an individual mentioned in paragraph (c) of subsection (2) except that, for the purposes of this subsection, the reference in that subsection to the registered person shall be construed as a reference to the Scottish Ministers or to a person nominated by them.".

(4)   In section 119(1) (sources of information), after the word "application" there is inserted "(whether for a certificate or for registration)".

(5)   After section 119 there is inserted—

"119A   Further sources of information: Scotland

(1)   Any person who holds, in Scotland, records of convictions for the use of police forces generally shall make those records available to the Scottish Ministers for the purpose of enabling them to carry out their functions under this Part in relation to the determination of whether a person should continue to be a person registered under section 120.

(2)   Where a person holds records of convictions or cautions for the use of police forces generally (but is not required by subsection (1) or section 119(1) to make those records available to the Scottish Ministers) the Scottish Ministers may request that person to make those records available to them; and they may also request that information kept under section 81(1) of the Care Standards Act 2000 (c.14) (duty of Secretary of State to keep list of individuals who are considered unsuitable to work with vulnerable adults) be made so available.

(3)   In subsection (1), "person" does not include—

   (a) a public body; or

   (b) a holder of a public office,

unless that person is a Scottish public authority (as defined in section 126(1) of the Scotland Act 1998 (c.46)).

(4) This section is without prejudice to section 119; and subsection (5) of that section shall apply in relation to records made available in accordance with this section as it does in relation to information made available in accordance with that section.".

(6) In section 120 (registered persons)—

(a) in subsection (2), after the words "Subject to" there is inserted "section 120A and"; and

(b) in subsection (3), after paragraph (a) there is inserted—

"(aa) the nomination by—

(i) a body corporate or unincorporate; or

(ii) a person appointed to an office by virtue of an enactment,

whether that body or person is registered or applying to be registered, of an individual to act for it or, as the case may be, him in relation to the countersigning of applications under this Part;

(ab) the refusal by the Scottish Ministers, on such grounds as may be specified in or determined under the regulations, to accept or to continue to accept any nomination made by virtue of this subsection;

(ac) as to the period which must elapse before any person refused registration or removed from the register may apply to be included in the register;".

(7) In section 122 (code of practice)—

(a) in subsection (1), after the words "provided to" there is inserted ", or the discharge of any function by,"; and

(b) after subsection (3) there is added—

"(4) Where the Scottish Ministers have reason to believe that—

(a) a registered person; or

(b) a body or individual at whose request a registered person has countersigned or is likely to countersign an application under section 113 or 115,

has failed to comply with the code of practice, they may remove the registered person from the register or impose conditions on him as respects his continuing to be listed in the register".

(8) After section 124 there is inserted—

"124A   Review of certain decisions as to registration

(1) Where the Scottish Ministers decide to refuse to include a person in the register maintained for the purposes of this Part or, other than by virtue of section 120(3)(b), to remove him from that register they shall notify him in writing of that decision and of their reason for so deciding and shall send a copy of that notification to the Secretary of State.

(2)   If the person considers that the information upon which the decision was based may have been inaccurate he may, by written notice to the Scottish Ministers setting out his reason for so considering, require them to review the decision; and they shall notify him in writing of the results of their review and of any consequential change in the decision and shall send a copy of—

      (a) the notice; and

      (b) the notification,

to the Secretary of State.

(3)   Any notification given by the Scottish Ministers under subsection (1) or (2) shall include information as to the provisions of any regulations made under section 120(3)(ac).

(4)   The Scottish Ministers may, for the purposes of this section, make regulations as to procedure; and such regulations may, in particular, make provision in relation to—

      (a) information to be included in any notification under subsection (1) or (2); and

      (b) the period within which—

            (i)   a requirement may be made under subsection (2); or

            (ii) a decision under subsection (1) is to be implemented.

124B **Scottish annotated list of certificated persons**

(1)   The Scottish Ministers shall maintain an annotated list for the purposes of this Part and shall include in that list all persons to whom a criminal record certificate, or as the case may be an enhanced criminal record certificate, has been issued under any of sections 113 to 116 of this Act.

(2)   The Scottish Ministers may make regulations about the maintenance of the list; and such regulations may, in particular, provide for—

      (a) the information to be included in the list;

      (b) the details to be provided, for the purposes of this section, by persons applying to be issued a criminal record certificate or enhanced criminal record certificate or countersigning any such application;

      (c) the procedure to be followed as respects the exercise of such discretion as is afforded them by subsection (3).

(3)   The Scottish Ministers may, as respects a person included in the list, if they are satisfied that it is appropriate to do so, notify the registered person who countersigned his application for the certificate in question (or on whose behalf that application was countersigned) or whomever else made the requisite statement which accompanied that application, about any relevant matter relating to the listed person ("relevant matter" having the same meaning as in section 113(5)) of which they become aware after issuing that certificate.

(4)   The Scottish Ministers are not to be satisfied as is mentioned in subsection (3) unless they are satisfied that the exempted question for the purpose of which the certificate was required remains relevant for the person to whom notification would, under that subsection, be given.

(5)   Regulations under paragraph (c) of subsection (2)—

(a) shall provide for there to be an opportunity for a listed person to make representations as respects whether the Scottish Ministers should be satisfied as is mentioned in subsection (3) and require them to have regard to those representations before giving notification under that subsection; and

(b) may require the person who would receive that notification (not being a person who is a Minister of the Crown) to provide them with such information as is in his possession and to which it would be appropriate for them to have regard as respects the exercise of the discretion mentioned in that paragraph.".

PART 11

LOCAL AUTHORITY FUNCTIONS

71   Advice, guidance and assistance to persons arrested or on whom sentence deferred

(1)   The Social Work (Scotland) Act 1968 (c.49) is amended as follows.

(2)   In subsection (1) of section 27 (which requires local authorities, among other things, to provide advice, guidance and assistance for persons in their area who are subject to supervision or treatment by virtue of a court order, enactment or licence or of a referral to a local authority in the absence of prosecution, who are subject to a community service or probation order or who are released from detention), after paragraph (ab) there is inserted—

"(ac) the provision of advice, guidance and assistance for persons who are in prison or subject to any other form of detention and who—

(i)   resided in their area immediately prior to such imprisonment or detention; or

(ii)   intend to reside in their area on release from such imprisonment or detention,

and who on release from such imprisonment or detention, it appears to the local authority, will be required to be under supervision under any enactment or by the terms of an order or licence of the Scottish Ministers or of a condition or requirement imposed in pursuance of an enactment;".

(3)   After that subsection there is inserted—

"(1A) A local authority may provide advice, guidance or assistance for any person who—

(a)   would fall to be provided for under paragraph (ac) of subsection (1) above but for the fact that it appears to the local authority that he will not be required to be under any form of supervision on release as mentioned in that paragraph; and

(b)   requests such advice, guidance or assistance.

(1B) Where as respects any person more than one local authority is required by paragraph (ac) of subsection (1) to make such provision as is mentioned in that paragraph, they may agree between themselves that only one of them shall do so; and where there is such agreement the paragraph shall apply accordingly.".

(4)   After that section there is inserted—

"27ZA Advice, guidance and assistance to persons arrested or on whom sentence deferred

(1) It shall be a function of a local authority, if and to such extent as the Scottish Ministers so direct and in accordance with the direction, to provide, directly or indirectly, advice, guidance and assistance to any person (and in particular to any person who appears to the local authority to have dependency problems)—

    (a) who is arrested and detained in police custody in their area, but only during the period of such detention; or

    (b) on whom sentence is deferred under section 202(1) of the 1995 Act, but only during the period of deferment and while that person is in their area.

(2) The function mentioned in subsection (1)(a) above may continue to be exercised by the local authority while the person is in their area for a period not exceeding 12 months from the date of his release from police custody.

(3) In subsection (1) above, "dependency problems" means problems relating to a dependency on drugs, alcohol or some other substance.".

(5) In paragraph (a) of section 27A(1) (which enables the Scottish Ministers to make grants to a local authority in respect of expenditure incurred by the authority for the purposes mentioned in section 27(1)), after the words "27(1)" there is inserted "or 27ZA".

72 Grants to local authorities discharging certain functions jointly

In section 27A of the Social Work (Scotland) Act 1968 (which enables the Scottish Ministers to make grants to a local authority in respect of expenditure incurred by the authority for purposes connected with the provision of reports in relation to offenders and with the supervision and care of certain persons subject to supervision or treatment by virtue of court order, enactment or licence or of referral to a local authority in the absence of prosecution), after subsection (1) there is inserted—

"(1A) In a case where two or more local authorities are discharging any function mentioned in section 27(1) or 27ZA of this Act jointly, whether or not in accordance with arrangements made under section 56(5) of the Local Government (Scotland) Act 1973 (c.65), the power of the Scottish Ministers to make grants under subsection (1) above in respect of expenditure incurred for the purposes mentioned in paragraph (a) of that subsection includes a power to make such grants, on such conditions as are mentioned in that subsection, to a local authority nominated by the local authorities from among their number.".

PART 12

MISCELLANEOUS AND GENERAL

Miscellaneous

73 Public defence

In section 28A of the Legal Aid (Scotland) Act 1986 (c.47) (power of Scottish Legal Aid Board directly to employ solicitors to provide criminal legal assistance)—

(a) subsections (2), (3) and (10) to (15) are repealed; and

(b) after subsection (9) there is added—

"(9A) Before 31st December 2008, the Scottish Ministers shall lay before the Parliament a report on the progress of the feasibility study.".

74   Offences aggravated by religious prejudice

(1)   This section applies where it is—

    (a)   libelled in an indictment; or

    (b)   specified in a complaint,

and, in either case, proved that an offence has been aggravated by religious prejudice.

(2)   For the purposes of this section, an offence is aggravated by religious prejudice if—

    (a)   at the time of committing the offence or immediately before or after doing so, the offender evinces towards the victim (if any) of the offence malice and ill-will based on the victim's membership (or presumed membership) of a religious group, or of a social or cultural group with a perceived religious affiliation; or

    (b)   the offence is motivated (wholly or partly) by malice and ill-will towards members of a religious group, or of a social or cultural group with a perceived religious affiliation, based on their membership of that group.

(3)   Where this section applies, the court must take the aggravation into account in determining the appropriate sentence.

(4)   Where the sentence in respect of the offence is different from that which the court would have imposed had the offence not been aggravated by religious prejudice, the court must state the extent of and the reasons for that difference.

(5)   For the purposes of this section, evidence from a single source is sufficient to prove that an offence is aggravated by religious prejudice.

(6)   In subsection (2)(a)—

    "membership" in relation to a group includes association with members of that group; and

    "presumed" means presumed by the offender.

(7)   In this section, "religious group" means a group of persons defined by reference to their—

    (a)   religious belief or lack of religious belief;

    (b)   membership of or adherence to a church or religious organisation;

    (c)   support for the culture and traditions of a church or religious organisation; or

    (d)   participation in activities associated with such a culture or such traditions.

75   Reintroduction of ranks of deputy chief constable and chief superintendent

(1)   The Police (Scotland) Act 1967 (c.77) is amended as follows.

(2)   For section 5 there is substituted—

    "5   Deputy and assistant chief constables

    (1)   Every police force shall have a deputy chief constable.

    (2)   The ranks which may be held in a police force shall include that of assistant chief constable.

(3) Appointments and promotions to the rank of deputy chief constable or assistant chief constable shall be made, in accordance with regulations under section 26 of this Act, by the police authority after consultation with the chief constable and subject to the approval of the Scottish Ministers.

(4) Subsections (4) to (7) of section 4 of this Act shall apply to a deputy chief constable or an assistant chief constable as they apply to a chief constable.

5A   Power of deputy or assistant chief constable to exercise functions of chief constable

(1) The deputy chief constable of a police force may exercise or perform any or all of the powers and duties of the chief constable of that force—

   (a) during any absence, incapacity or suspension from duty of the chief constable;

   (b) during any vacancy in the office of the chief constable; or

   (c) at any other time, with the consent of the chief constable.

(2) A person holding the rank of assistant chief constable in a police force may be designated by the police authority to exercise or perform any or all of the powers and duties of the chief constable of that force during—

   (a) any absence, incapacity or suspension from duty of; or

   (b) any vacancy in the offices of,

   both the chief constable and the deputy chief constable.

(3) Only one person shall be authorised to act at any one time by virtue of a designation under subsection (2) above.

(4) Exercise for a continuous period of more than three months of any power conferred by virtue of subsection (1)(a) or (b) or (2) above shall require the consent of the Scottish Ministers.

(5) The provisions of subsections (1) and (2) above shall be without prejudice to any other enactment which makes provision for the exercise by any other person of powers conferred on a chief constable.".

(3) In section 7(1) (ranks), after the words—

   (a) "of chief constable" there is inserted ", deputy chief constable"; and

   (b) "assistant chief constable" there is inserted ", chief superintendent".

(4) In section 26(2A)(b) (regulations as to dismissal etc. of constable holding a rank above that of superintendent), after the words "that of" there is inserted "chief".

(5) In section 31 (powers of Scottish Ministers in relation to compulsory retirement of chief constable or assistant chief constable)—

   (a) in subsection (2)—

      (i) after the words "with respect to" there is inserted "the deputy or"; and

      (ii) for the words "chief constable or assistant chief constable" there is substituted "officer in respect of whom the power is to be exercised"; and

   (b) in subsection (4), after the words "a chief constable" there is inserted "or deputy".

76   Police custody and security officers

(1)   The Police (Scotland) Act 1967 (c.77) is amended as follows.

(2)   In section 9 (civilian employees)—

>   (a)   in subsection (1), the existing words from "employ" to the end become paragraph (a) and after that paragraph there is inserted the word "; or" and the following paragraph—

>>   "(b)   appoint for such purposes as such officers persons provided under a contract for services entered into by the authority with some other person";

>   (b)   after that subsection there is inserted—

>   "(1A) The category of persons—

>>   (a)   so employed or appointed; and

>>   (b)   in respect of each of whom there is for the time being a certificate in force, certifying that he has been approved by the chief constable for the purposes of performing functions in relation to custody and security and is accordingly authorised to perform them for the police force,

>   shall be known as the police authority's "police custody and security officers".

>   (1B) Without prejudice to powers or duties which a police custody and security officer may have under or by virtue of any other enactment, for the purposes of the functions which he is authorised to perform by virtue of subsection (1A)(b) above, any such officer shall have the powers mentioned in subsection (1C) below and the duties mentioned in subsection (1E) below; except that no officer provided as is mentioned in subsection (1)(b) above shall have those powers and duties in the premises of any court or in land connected with such premises.

>   (1C) The powers are—

>>   (a)   to transfer persons in legal custody from one set of relevant premises to another;

>>   (b)   to have custody of persons held in legal custody on court premises (whether or not such persons would otherwise be in the custody of the court) and to produce them before the court;

>>   (c)   to have custody of persons temporarily held in legal custody in relevant premises while in the course of transfer from one set of such premises to another;

>>   (d)   to apprehend a person who was in the custody of the officer in relevant premises or in such course of transfer but who is unlawfully at large;

>>   (e)   to remove from relevant premises any person—

>>>   (i)   who he has reasonable grounds to believe has committed or is committing an offence; or

>>>   (ii)   who is causing a disturbance or nuisance;

>>   (f)   in any place to search any person who is in legal custody or is unlawfully at large;

(g) in relevant premises, or in any other place in which a person in his custody who is being transferred from one set of relevant premises to another is present, to search (any or all)—

    (i) property;

    (ii) any person who he has reasonable grounds to believe has committed or is committing an offence;

    (iii) any person who is seeking access to a person in the officer's custody or to relevant premises;

(h) in relevant premises, or in any other place in which a person in legal custody is or may be, to require any person who he has reasonable grounds for suspecting has committed or is committing an offence to give his name and address and either—

    (i) to remain there with the officer until the arrival of a constable; or

    (ii) where reasonable in all the circumstances, to go with the officer to the nearest police station,

but only if before imposing any such requirement on a person the officer informs him of the nature of the suspected offence and of the reason for the requirement;

(i) in fulfilment of his duties under subsection (1E)(d) below, to apprehend any person and to detain that person in custody in the premises of the court in question;

(j) at a constable's direction, to photograph, or take relevant physical data from, any person held in legal custody; and

(k) to use reasonable force (which may include the use of handcuffs and other means of restraint) where and in so far as it is requisite to do so in exercising any of the other powers.

(1D) In subsection (1C) above—

"legal custody" has the meaning given by section 295 of the Criminal Procedure (Scotland) Act 1995 (c.46);

"relevant physical data" has the meaning given by section 18(7A) of that Act; and

"relevant premises" means—

    (a) the premises of any court, prison, police station or hospital (within the meaning of the Mental Health (Scotland) Act 1984 (c.36)); or

    (b) the premises of any other place from or to which a person may be required to be taken under that Act of 1984 or that Act of 1995,

and either (but not both) of the sets of premises mentioned in any of paragraphs (a), (c) and (g) of that subsection may be situated in a part of the British Islands outwith Scotland.

(1E) The duties are—

    (a) to attend to the well-being of persons in their custody;

    (b) to prevent the escape of such persons from their custody;

    (c) to prevent, or detect and report on, the commission or attempted commission by such persons of other unlawful acts;

    (d) to act with a view to preserving good order in the premises of any court and in land connected with such premises;

    (e) to ensure good order and discipline on the part of such persons (whether or not in the premises of any court or in land connected with such premises); and

    (f) to give effect to any order of a court.

  (1F) A police custody and security officer is not to be regarded as acting in accordance with those powers and duties at any time when not readily identifiable as such an officer (whether or not by means of a uniform or badge worn).";

  (c) in subsection (2), after the word "employed" there is inserted ", or appointed,"; and

  (d) in subsection (3)—

    (i) after the word "employed" there is inserted ", or appointed,"; and

    (ii) after the words "by the authority" there is inserted "(not being police custody and security officers)".

(3) After section 9 there is inserted—

"9A   Certification of police custody and security officers

(1) A chief constable may, on the application of any person employed or appointed by his police authority, issue in respect of that person a certificate such as is mentioned in section 9(1A)(b) of this Act.

(2) The chief constable shall not do so unless satisfied that the applicant—

    (a) is a fit and proper person to perform for the police force the functions of a police custody and security officer; and

    (b) has received training to such standard as the chief constable considers appropriate for the performance of those functions.

(3) A certificate so issued shall, subject to any suspension under paragraph (a) of subsection (4) below or revocation under paragraph (b) of that subsection, continue in force until such date or occurrence as may be specified in the certificate.

(4) If at any time it appears to the chief constable that the person in respect of whom the certificate has been issued—

    (a) may not be a fit and proper person to perform the functions of a police custody and security officer he may suspend (pending his consideration of whether to proceed under paragraph (b) of this subsection);

    (b) is not a fit and proper person to perform those functions he may revoke,

the certificate and such authorisation as it confers.

9B   **False statements in relation to certification**

A person who, for the purpose of obtaining a certificate such as is mentioned in section 9(1A)(b) of this Act for himself or any other person—

     (a)   makes a statement which he knows to be; or

     (b)   recklessly makes a statement which is,

false in a material particular, shall be guilty of an offence and liable on summary conviction to a fine not exceeding level 4 on the standard scale.".

(4)   In section 39 (liability for wrongful acts of constables)—

     (a)   in subsection (1), after the words "any constable" there is inserted "or police custody and security officer";

     (b)   in subsection (4), after the words "Police Act 1997" there is inserted "or any police custody and security officer employed or appointed by them"; and

     (c)   at the end there is added—

     "(5)   This section is without prejudice to any obligation or indemnity arising by virtue of a contract entered into under section 9(1)(b) of this Act.".

(5)   In section 41 (assaults on constables etc.)—

     (a)   in subsection (1)(a), after the word "constable" where it occurs for—

         (i)   the first time there is inserted "or police custody and security officer"; and

         (ii)   the second time there is inserted "or any such officer"; and

     (b)   in subsection (2), after the words—

         (i)   "custody of a constable" there is inserted "or police custody and security officer"; and

         (ii)   "assisting a constable" there is inserted "or any such officer".

(6)   In section 43 (impersonation etc.)—

     (a)   in subsection (1)(a), after the word "constable" there is inserted "or police custody and security officer"; and

     (b)   in subsection (3), after the word "constables" there is inserted "or police custody and security officers".

(7)   In section 44 (offences by constables)—

     (a)   in subsection (2), after the words "Any constable" there is inserted "or police custody and security officer";

     (b)   in subsection (3), after the words "Any constable" there is inserted "or any such officer"; and

     (c)   in subsection (4), after the words "a constable", in each of the two places they occur, there is inserted "or such an officer".

(8)   In section 45 (warrant to search for police accoutrements and clothing), after the words "a constable" there is inserted "or a police custody and security officer".

(9)   In section 51(1) (interpretation), at the appropriate place there is inserted—

     ""police custody and security officer" shall be construed in accordance with section 9(1A) of this Act;".

determine that, in the interests of justice, the arrangements shall not be continued with and postpone the diet, or as the case may be the hearing or examination, to the next day which is not a Saturday, Sunday or court holiday prescribed for the court.

(4)   The period of any such postponement is not to count towards any time limit applying in respect of the case.

(5)   Paragraph (a)(ii) of subsection (1) does not apply where, in relation to an application under that subsection, the court is satisfied that neither (or as the case may be none) of the parties intends to lead or present, at the diet mentioned in that paragraph, evidence as to the charge.

81   Warrants issued in Northern Ireland for search of premises in Scotland

(1)   Where a warrant issued by a magistrate or county court judge in Northern Ireland for the search of premises in Scotland is duly endorsed by a sheriff or justice of the peace in whose jurisdiction the warrant purports to authorise search, the warrant has effect as if granted by the sheriff or, as the case may be, justice of the peace.

(2)   The reference in subsection (1) to the warrant being duly endorsed is to its being endorsed in the manner specified in subsection (1) of section 4 of the Summary Jurisdiction (Process) Act 1881 (c.24) as if it were a process mentioned in that subsection.

82   Use of electronic communications or electronic storage in connection with warrants to search

(1)   This section, which is without prejudice to section 8 of the Electronic Communications Act 2000 (c.7) (power to modify legislation), applies to warrants to search granted under section 134(1) of the 1995 Act (that is to say, where incidental to proceedings by complaint or although no subsequent proceedings by complaint may follow).

(2)   Subject to subsections (1) and (4), the Scottish Ministers may, in relation to warrants to which this section applies, by order modify—

    (a)   any rule of law; or

    (b)   the practice and procedure in relation to criminal proceedings,

in such manner as they think fit so as to authorise or facilitate the use of electronic communications or electronic storage (instead of other forms of communication or storage) for any purpose mentioned in subsection (3).

(3)   Those purposes are (in relation to the rule of law or the practice and procedure) the purposes mentioned (in relation to the provisions which may be modified under subsection (1) of section 8 of that Act of 2000) in any of paragraphs (a) to (f) of subsection (2) of that section.

(4)   The Scottish Ministers are not to make an order under subsection (2) authorising the use of electronic communications or electronic storage for any purpose unless they consider that the authorisation is such that the extent (if any) to which records of things done for that purpose will be available will be no less satisfactory in cases where use is made of electronic communications or electronic storage than in other cases.

(5)   Subsections (4) to (6) and (8) of section 8 and (5) and (6) of section 9 of that Act of 2000 apply in relation to an order made under subsection (2) as they apply in relation to an order made under subsection (1) of the said section 8.

(b) summoned by virtue of section 12 of the Court of Session Act 1988 (c.36) (summoning of jury),

before that date is not, by virtue of subsection (1), excused from attending in compliance with the citation or disqualified from serving as a juror at the sitting, or trial, in question.

79   Separation of jury after retiral

It shall no longer be mandatory for the period during which a jury, after retiring to consider their verdict, are enclosed to be continuous; and accordingly, in section 99 of the 1995 Act (seclusion of jury to consider verdict)—

(a) in subsection (1), for the word "after" there is substituted "while";

(b) in subsection (2), for the words "until the jury" there is substituted "while the jury are enclosed and until they";

(c) in subsection (4)(b), after the word "and" there is inserted ", unless under subsection (7) below the court permits them to separate,"; and

(d) at the end there is added—

"(7)   The court may, if it thinks fit, permit the jury to separate even after they have retired to consider their verdict.".

80   Television link from court to prison or other place of detention

(1) In proceedings in the High Court or sheriff court the court may, on application to it, make in relation to—

(a) any diet other than—

(i) the first calling of the case in a summary prosecution; or

(ii) a diet at which evidence as to the charge may be led or presented;

(b) the hearing, on an occasion other than a first occasion such as is mentioned in section 22A(1) of the 1995 Act (which relates to first appearance), of a petition under section 34(1) of that Act (petition for warrant); or

(c) any judicial examination conducted, other than on such a first occasion, by virtue of such a petition,

arrangements whereby any due participation, at the diet, hearing or examination, of an accused who is a person imprisoned, or detained, in any place in Scotland is through a live television link from that place, the accused not being brought to the court-room or as the case may be to chambers; but this subsection is subject to subsection (5).

(2) Where such arrangements are made the place is, for the purposes of the proceedings, to be deemed part of the court-room or as the case may be of chambers and any proceedings conducted in accordance with the arrangements are to be deemed to take place in the presence of the accused.

(3) The court—

(a) may at any time before or during the diet, hearing or examination; and

(b) in the case of a diet, must, where the arrangements were made by virtue of subsection (5) but at the diet a party seeks duly to lead or present evidence as to the charge,

CASES CALLING VIA LIVE T.V. LINK FROM BARLINNIE

◆ At the first calling the procurator fiscal will move to have the case call for full committal by way of the live link from Barlinnie, in terms of s 80 of The Criminal Justice Scotland Act 2003.

◆ All clients appearing over the link will have access to their agent ,(via the link), prior to the case calling in court.

◆ This meeting will be initiated by the agent by calling the agent co- ordinator at Barlinnie on the following number :-

◆ 0141-770-2094

◆   Booths 2 and 3 will be left vacant between 11.30 am and 1.30pm on the day the case is due to call for full committal.

Criminal Justice (Scotland) Act 2003

2003 asp 7

ISBN 0 10 590049 4

CORRECTION

Page 74 –

<u>Section **76** (4)(c)</u>

Amend reference to new subsection "(5)" to read new subsection "(8)"

September 2003

PRINTED IN THE UNITED KINGDOM BY THE STATIONERY OFFICE LIMITED
under the authority and superintendence of Carol Tullo, the Queen's Printer for Scotland

(10) In section 102(5) of the Criminal Justice and Public Order Act 1994 (c33) (compliance with warrants or orders), at the end there is added "or by a police custody and security officer in the performance of functions prescribed under section 9(1A)(b) of the Police (Scotland) Act 1967 (c.77)".

(11) In section 307(1) of the 1995 Act (interpretation), in paragraph (c) of the definition of "officer of law"—

   (a) after the word "employed" there is inserted "or appointed";

   (b) after the words "and who" there is inserted "either"; and

   (c) at the end there is added "or is a police custody and security officer".

77 Wildlife offences

Schedule 3 to this Act, which contains amendments to the Wildlife and Countryside Act 1981 (c.69) relating to penalties for, and powers of arrest as regards, offences under Part I of that Act, has effect.

78 Disqualification from jury service

(1) In Schedule 1 to the Law Reform (Miscellaneous Provisions) (Scotland) Act 1980 (c.55) (ineligibility for and disqualification and excusal from jury service), in Part II, after paragraph (b) there is inserted—

   "(bb) persons who have been convicted of an offence if, in respect of the conviction, one or more of the following orders was made—

     (i) a probation order under section 228(1) of the Criminal Procedure (Scotland) Act 1995 (c.46) (section 247 of that Act being disregarded for the purposes of this head);

     (ii) a drug treatment and testing order under section 234B(2) of that Act;

     (iii) a community service order under section 238(1) of that Act;

     (iv) a restriction of liberty order under section 245A(1) of that Act;

     (v) a community order as defined by section 33(1) of the Powers of Criminal Courts (Sentencing) Act 2000 (c.6);

     (vi) a community order as defined by article 2(2) of the Criminal Justice (Northern Ireland) Order 1996 (SI 1996/3160 (N.I.24));

     (vii) a drug treatment and testing order under article 8(2) of the Criminal Justice (Northern Ireland) Order 1998 (SI 1998/2839 (N.I.20)),

   except where they are rehabilitated persons for the purposes of the Rehabilitation of Offenders Act 1974 (c.53);".

(2) Subject to subsection (3), the insertion made by subsection (1) has effect even in relation to a case where the probation order, drug treatment and testing order, community service order, restriction of liberty order or community order is made before the date on which subsection (1) is brought into force.

(3) A person—

   (a) cited under section 85(4) of the 1995 Act (citation of jurors); or

(b) summoned by virtue of section 12 of the Court of Session Act 1988 (c.36) (summoning of jury),

before that date is not, by virtue of subsection (1), excused from attending in compliance with the citation or disqualified from serving as a juror at the sitting, or trial, in question.

79   Separation of jury after retiral

It shall no longer be mandatory for the period during which a jury, after retiring to consider their verdict, are enclosed to be continuous; and accordingly, in section 99 of the 1995 Act (seclusion of jury to consider verdict)—

(a) in subsection (1), for the word "after" there is substituted "while";

(b) in subsection (2), for the words "until the jury" there is substituted "while the jury are enclosed and until they";

(c) in subsection (4)(b), after the word "and" there is inserted ", unless under subsection (7) below the court permits them to separate,"; and

(d) at the end there is added—

"(7)   The court may, if it thinks fit, permit the jury to separate even after they have retired to consider their verdict.".

80   Television link from court to prison or other place of detention

(1) In proceedings in the High Court or sheriff court the court may, on application to it, make in relation to—

(a) any diet other than—

(i)   the first calling of the case in a summary prosecution; or

(ii) a diet at which evidence as to the charge may be led or presented;

(b) the hearing, on an occasion other than a first occasion such as is mentioned in section 22A(1) of the 1995 Act (which relates to first appearance), of a petition under section 34(1) of that Act (petition for warrant); or

(c) any judicial examination conducted, other than on such a first occasion, by virtue of such a petition,

arrangements whereby any due participation, at the diet, hearing or examination, of an accused who is a person imprisoned, or detained, in any place in Scotland is through a live television link from that place, the accused not being brought to the court-room or as the case may be to chambers; but this subsection is subject to subsection (5).

(2) Where such arrangements are made the place is, for the purposes of the proceedings, to be deemed part of the court-room or as the case may be of chambers and any proceedings conducted in accordance with the arrangements are to be deemed to take place in the presence of the accused.

(3) The court—

(a) may at any time before or during the diet, hearing or examination; and

(b) in the case of a diet, must, where the arrangements were made by virtue of subsection (5) but at the diet a party seeks duly to lead or present evidence as to the charge, determine that, in the interests of justice, the arrangements shall not be continued with and postpone the diet, or as the case may be the hearing or examination, to the next day which is not a Saturday, Sunday or court holiday prescribed for the court.

(4)   The period of any such postponement is not to count towards any time limit applying in respect of the case.

(5)   Paragraph (a)(ii) of subsection (1) does not apply where, in relation to an application under that subsection, the court is satisfied that neither (or as the case may be none) of the parties intends to lead or present, at the diet mentioned in that paragraph, evidence as to the charge.

81   Warrants issued in Northern Ireland for search of premises in Scotland

(1)   Where a warrant issued by a magistrate or county court judge in Northern Ireland for the search of premises in Scotland is duly endorsed by a sheriff or justice of the peace in whose jurisdiction the warrant purports to authorise search, the warrant has effect as if granted by the sheriff or, as the case may be, justice of the peace.

(2)   The reference in subsection (1) to the warrant being duly endorsed is to its being endorsed in the manner specified in subsection (1) of section 4 of the Summary Jurisdiction (Process) Act 1881 (c.24) as if it were a process mentioned in that subsection.

82   Use of electronic communications or electronic storage in connection with warrants to search

(1)   This section, which is without prejudice to section 8 of the Electronic Communications Act 2000 (c.7) (power to modify legislation), applies to warrants to search granted under section 134(1) of the 1995 Act (that is to say, where incidental to proceedings by complaint or although no subsequent proceedings by complaint may follow).

(2)   Subject to subsections (1) and (4), the Scottish Ministers may, in relation to warrants to which this section applies, by order modify—

    (a)   any rule of law; or

    (b)   the practice and procedure in relation to criminal proceedings,

in such manner as they think fit so as to authorise or facilitate the use of electronic communications or electronic storage (instead of other forms of communication or storage) for any purpose mentioned in subsection (3).

(3)   Those purposes are (in relation to the rule of law or the practice and procedure) the purposes mentioned (in relation to the provisions which may be modified under subsection (1) of section 8 of that Act of 2000) in any of paragraphs (a) to (f) of subsection (2) of that section.

(4)   The Scottish Ministers are not to make an order under subsection (2) authorising the use of electronic communications or electronic storage for any purpose unless they consider that the authorisation is such that the extent (if any) to which records of things done for that purpose will be available will be no less satisfactory in cases where use is made of electronic communications or electronic storage than in other cases.

(5)   Subsections (4) to (6) and (8) of section 8 and (5) and (6) of section 9 of that Act of 2000 apply in relation to an order made under subsection (2) as they apply in relation to an order made under subsection (1) of the said section 8.

(6)   Expressions used in this section and in that Act of 2000 have the same meanings in this section as in that Act.

83   Anti-social behaviour strategies

In the Crime and Disorder Act 1998 (c.37), after section 22 (offences in relation to breach of anti-social behaviour orders) there is inserted—

    "**22A   Anti–social behaviour strategies**

(1)   Each local authority shall prepare jointly with the relevant chief constable a strategy for dealing with anti-social behaviour in the authority's area; and the authority shall publish the strategy.

(2)   The strategy shall, in particular, include provision as to—

    (a) how the authority and the police are to co-ordinate the exercise of their functions in so far as they are exercisable in relation to anti-social behaviour in the authority's area; and

    (b) the exchange of information between the authority and the police relating to such behaviour.

(3)   The local authority and the relevant chief constable—

    (a) shall keep the strategy under review; and

    (b) may from time to time revise the strategy,

and the authority shall publish the strategy as so revised.

(4)   In this section—

    "anti-social behaviour" means any act or conduct (including speech) which causes or is likely to cause alarm, distress, nuisance or annoyance to any person;

    "local authority" means a council constituted under section 2 of the Local Government etc. (Scotland) Act 1994 (c.39) and any reference to the area of such an authority is a reference to the local government area within the meaning of that Act for which it is so constituted;

    "relevant chief constable" means the chief constable of the police force maintained under the Police (Scotland) Act 1967 (c.77) the area of which includes the area of the local authority.".

General

84   Transitional provisions etc.

(1)   The Scottish Ministers may by order make such incidental, supplemental, consequential, transitional, transitory or saving provision as they consider necessary or expedient for the purposes, or in consequence, of this Act or of any order made under this Act.

(2)   An order under subsection (1) above may amend or repeal any enactment (including any provision of this Act).

85   Minor and consequential amendments

Schedule 4 to this Act, which contains minor amendments and amendments consequential on the provisions of this Act, has effect.

86   Repeals

The enactments mentioned in schedule 5 to this Act are repealed to the extent mentioned in the second column of that schedule.

87   Interpretation

(1)   In this Act—

"the 1989 Act" means the Prisons (Scotland) Act 1989 (c.45);

"the 1993 Act" means the Prisoners and Criminal Proceedings (Scotland) Act 1993 (c.9);

"the 1995 Act" means the Criminal Procedure (Scotland) Act 1995 (c.46); and

"prescribed", except in section 21(4), means prescribed by order made by the Scottish Ministers.

(2)   Any expression used in this Act and in the 1995 Act is, unless the context requires otherwise, to be construed in accordance with section 307 of that Act (interpretation).

88   Orders

(1)   Any power of the Scottish Ministers to make orders or regulations under this Act is exercisable by statutory instrument; and subject to subsection (2) a statutory instrument containing any such order or regulations, other than an order under section 89(2), is subject to annulment in pursuance of a resolution of the Parliament.

(2)   A statutory instrument containing an order under section—

(a) 6(1)(b), 11(1), 14(1), 14(12) (including as applied to section 16(5)), 16(4) or 42(5); or

(b) 84 which amends or repeals any part of an Act,

is not made unless a draft of the instrument has been laid before, and approved by resolution of, the Parliament.

89   Short title and commencement

(1)   This Act may be cited as the Criminal Justice (Scotland) Act 2003.

(2)   With the exception of—

(a) this section;

(b) section 77 and schedule 3;

(c) section 84;

(d) in so far as relating to the Wildlife and Countryside Act 1981 (c.69), section 86 and schedule 5;

(e) section 87; and

(f) section 88,

this Act comes into force on such day as the Scottish Ministers may by order appoint.

(3)   Different days may be so appointed for different provisions and for different purposes.

SCHEDULE 1
(introduced by section 1(2))

ORDER FOR LIFELONG RESTRICTION: MODIFICATION OF ENACTMENTS

Prisoners and Criminal Proceedings (Scotland) Act 1993 (c.9)

1 (1) The 1993 Act is amended in accordance with this paragraph.

(2) In section 2 (duty to release discretionary life prisoners)—

(a) in subsection (1), after paragraph (aa) there is inserted "or

(ab) who is subject to an order for lifelong restriction in respect of an offence,";

(b) in subsection (2)(aa)—

(i) after the words "paragraph (a)" there is inserted "or (ab)"; and

(ii) in sub-paragraph (i), after the word "life" there is inserted ", or as the case may be not made the order for lifelong restriction,";

(c) in subsection (3), after the words "subsection (1) above" there is inserted "or makes an order for lifelong restriction";

(d) after subsection (9) there is added—

"(10) In subsection (9) above, the reference to "sentences of imprisonment for life" is to be construed as including a reference to any sentence constituted by an order for lifelong restriction.".

(3) In section 27(1) (interpretation)—

(a) in the definition of "life prisoner", at the end there is added "or in respect of whom there has been made an order for lifelong restriction"; and

(b) the following definitions are inserted at the appropriate places—

""order for lifelong restriction" means an order under section 210F(1) of the Criminal Procedure (Scotland) Act 1995 (c.46);"

""risk management plan" shall be construed in accordance with section 6(1) of the Criminal Justice (Scotland) Act 2003 (asp 7);".

Criminal Procedure (Scotland) Act 1995 (c.46)

2 (1) The 1995 Act is amended in accordance with this paragraph.

(2) In section 69 (notice of previous convictions)—

(a) after subsection (4) there is inserted—

"(4A) A notice served under subsection (2) or (4) above shall include any details which the prosecutor proposes to provide under section 101(3A) of this Act; and subsection (3) above shall apply in relation to intimation objecting to the provision of such details, on the grounds that they do not apply to the accused or are otherwise inadmissible, as it applies in relation to intimation objecting to a conviction."; and

(b) in subsection (5), after the word "section" there is inserted ", or to the provision of such details as are, by virtue of subsection (4A) above, included in a notice so served,".

(3)   In section 101 (previous convictions: solemn proceedings)—

    (a)   in subsection (3), the existing words "for sentence" become paragraph (a); and after that paragraph there is inserted the word "; or" and the following paragraph—

        "(b) for a risk assessment order (or the court at its own instance proposes to make such an order)"; and

    (b)   after that subsection there is inserted—

        "(3A) Where, under paragraph (b) of subsection (3) above, the prosecutor lays previous convictions before the judge, he shall also provide the judge with such details regarding the offences in question as are available to him.".

(4)   In section 106(1) (right of appeal), after paragraph (b) there is inserted—

        "(ba) against the making of an order for lifelong restriction;".

(5)   In section 195(1) (sheriff's duty in certain circumstances to remit convicted person to High Court for sentence), after—

    (a)   the word "inadequate" there is inserted "or it appears to him that the criteria mentioned in section 210E of this Act (that is to say, the risk criteria) may be met"; and

    (b)   the words "so that" there is inserted ", in either case,".

(6)   In section 204(2A) (restrictions on passing sentence of imprisonment or detention), after the word "court" there is inserted ", unless it has made a risk assessment order in respect of the person,".

(7)   In section 307(1) (interpretation), the following definitions are inserted at the appropriate places—

        ""order for lifelong restriction" means an order under section 210F(1) of this Act;"

        ""risk assessment order" means an order under section 210B(2) of this Act;"

        ""risk assessment report" has the meaning given by section 210B(3)(a) of this Act;".

SCHEDULE 2
(introduced by section 3(3))

CONSTITUTION ETC. OF THE RISK MANAGEMENT AUTHORITY

Status

1   The Risk Management Authority ("the Authority") is a body corporate.

2   The Authority—

    (a) is not a servant or agent of the Crown; and

    (b) has no status, immunity or privilege of the Crown,

and its property is not to be regarded as property of, or held on behalf of, the Crown.

Membership

3 (1) The Authority consists of such members (including a convener) as the Scottish Ministers may appoint.

   (2) Each member—

    (a) is appointed for such period, not exceeding 5 years, as is specified in the terms of the appointment;

    (b) holds and vacates office in accordance with those terms;

    (c) is eligible for reappointment but may not hold office for a period exceeding 10 years in aggregate;

    (d) may, by written notice to the Scottish Ministers, resign membership.

   (3) The Scottish Ministers may remove a member from office if they are satisfied that the member—

    (a) without reasonable excuse, has not complied with the terms of the appointment;

    (b) is otherwise unable or unfit to discharge the functions of member or is unsuitable to continue as a member.

Procedure

4 (1) The Authority may regulate its own procedure (including any quorum).

   (2) The validity of any proceedings of the Authority is not affected by any vacancy in membership nor any defect in the appointment of a member.

Remuneration, allowances and pensions

5 (1) The Authority may, with the approval of the Scottish Ministers, pay—

    (a) such remuneration and allowances to its members; and

    (b) in respect of any office held by a person as member—

      (i) such pension, allowance or gratuity to or in respect of the person; and

      (ii) such contribution or other payment towards provision of such pension, allowance or gratuity,

as it may with such approval determine.

   (2) Where a person ceases to be a member otherwise than on expiry of term of office, the Authority may, exceptionally and with the approval of the Scottish Ministers, pay to the person such amount by way of compensation for loss of office as it may with such approval determine.

Staff

6 (1) The Authority may, with the approval of the Scottish Ministers, appoint such employees as it considers are required on such terms and conditions as it may with such approval determine.

   (2) The authority is to—

    (a) pay such pensions, allowances and gratuities to or in respect of its employees or former employees;

(b) make such payment towards provision of such pensions, allowances or gratuities; and

(c) provide and maintain such schemes (whether contributory or not) for the payment of such pensions, allowances and gratuities,

as it may with the approval of the Scottish Ministers determine.

(3) References in sub-paragraph (2) to pensions, allowances or gratuities include their provision by way of compensation for loss of office or employment.

SCHEDULE 3
(introduced by section 77)

WILDLIFE OFFENCES

1   The Wildlife and Countryside Act 1981 (c.69) is amended in accordance with the following paragraphs.

2   In each of sections 6(8) (regulations as to dealing in dead wild birds etc. after having been convicted of an offence under Part I of the Act) and 7(3) (keeping or possessing certain birds after having been so convicted), for paragraphs (a) and (b) there is substituted "within five years of his having been convicted of—

(a) an offence under this Part (being an offence relating to the protection of birds or other animals); or

(b) any other offence involving their ill-treatment,".

3   In section 7(4) (offence relating to disposal etc. of certain birds), for paragraphs (a) and (b) there is substituted "within five years of that person's having been convicted of such an offence as is mentioned in subsection (3),".

4   In section 19 (enforcement)—

(a) in subsection (1)(c), the words "if he fails to give his name and address to the constable's satisfaction" are repealed; and

(b) in subsection (3), for paragraphs (a) and (b) there is substituted "an offence under this Part".

5   In section 20 (summary prosecutions)—

(a) subsection (1) is repealed; and

(b) in subsection (2), for the words "to which this section applies" there is substituted "under this Part".

6   In section 21 (penalties, forfeitures etc.)—

(a) for subsection (1) there is substituted—

"(1)   Subject to subsection (5), a person guilty of an offence under any of sections 1 to 13 or section 17 shall be liable on summary conviction to imprisonment for a term not exceeding six months or to a fine not exceeding level 5 on the standard scale, or to both.";

(b) subsections (2) and (3) are repealed;

(c) in subsection (4), for paragraphs (a) and (b) there is substituted—

"(a) on summary conviction, to imprisonment for a term not exceeding six months or to a fine not exceeding the statutory maximum, or to both;

(b) on conviction on indictment, to imprisonment for a term not exceeding two years or to a fine, or to both."; and

(d) in subsection (5), the words "(2) or (3)" are repealed.

SCHEDULE 4
(introduced by section 85)

MINOR AND CONSEQUENTIAL AMENDMENTS

Prisons (Scotland) Act 1989 (c.45)

1   Section 42 of the 1989 Act (exercise of powers to make rules, orders, etc.) is amended for the purposes of the existing provisions, within the meaning of Schedule 6 to the 1993 Act, as follows—

(a) in subsection (1), for the words "section 22(1A) or (2), 28(1A) or 37(1)" there is substituted "section 22(2) or 37(1)"; and

(b) in subsection (4), for the words "section 22(1A) or (2), 28(1A) of this Act" there is substituted "section 22(2) of this Act".

Prisoners and Criminal Proceedings (Scotland) Act 1993 (c.9)

2 (1)   The 1993 Act is amended as follows.

(2)   In section 1A (application of that Act to persons serving more than one sentence), in paragraph (c)(ii), after the word "specified" there is inserted "under".

(3)   In section 10 (life prisoners transferred to Scotland)—

(a) in subsection (2B), after paragraph (b) there are added the words "and in such a case subsection (3) below applies"; and

(b) in subsection (3)—

(i) after the word "applies" there is inserted "(whether by virtue of subsection (2) above or of subsection (2B) above)"; and

(ii) at the end, there are added the words "or as the case may be in the certificate or direction referred to in subsection (2D) above".

(4)   In section 45(3) (exercise of powers to make rules and orders), the words "or (6), 20(3)" are repealed.

Criminal Procedure (Scotland) Act 1995 (c.46)

3 (1)   The 1995 Act is amended as follows.

(2)   In each of sections 17A(1)(a) (right of person accused of sexual offence to be told about restriction on conduct of defence: arrest), 35(4A)(a) (judicial examination of accused), 66(6A)(a)(i) (citation and service of indictment), 140(2A)(a) (citation of accused in summary prosecution), 144(3A)(a) (procedure at first summary diet) and 146(3A)(a) (procedure in summary prosecution following not guilty plea), after the word "defence" there is added "and any proof ordered as is mentioned in section 288C(1) of this Act".

(3)   In section 220(1) (reduction in term of imprisonment by part payment of fine), after the word "imprisonment", where it first appears, there is inserted "imposed under section 219 of this Act in respect of the fine".

Crime and Punishment (Scotland) Act 1997 (c.48)

4   In Schedule 1 to the Crime and Punishment (Scotland) Act 1997, in paragraph 21(29), for the words "(5)" and "(6)" there is substituted "(6)" and "(7)" respectively.

Convention Rights (Compliance) (Scotland) Act 2001 (asp 7)

5   In the schedule to the Convention Rights (Compliance) (Scotland) Act 2001—

(a) in paragraph 16, for the words "transferred life prisoner" there is substituted "existing life prisoner"; and

(b) in paragraph 19, for the word "subsection" there is substituted "paragraph".

SCHEDULE 5
(introduced by section 86)

REPEALS

Enactment	Extent of repeal
Wildlife and Countryside Act 1981 (c.69)	In section 1, subsection (4); and in subsection (5) the words "and liable to a special penalty".
	In section 3(1), paragraph (c).
	In section 5(1), the words "and be liable to a special penalty".
	Section 6(4).
	In section 7(1), the words "and be liable to a special penalty".
	In section 8, in each of subsections (1) and (3), the words "and be liable to a special penalty".
Prisons (Scotland) Act 1989 (c.45)	Section 23.
Prisoners and Criminal Proceedings (Scotland) Act 1993 (c.9)	In section 2(1), the words "subject to subsection (9)(a) below and".

Enactment	Extent of repeal
Criminal Justice and Public Order Act 1994 (c.33)	Section 134(4).
Crime and Punishment (Scotland) Act 1997 (c.48)	Section 16(4).

Printed in the UK by The Stationery Office Limited
under the authority and superintendence of Carol Tullo, the Queen's Printer for Scotland